# ECDL® 5.0

## European Computer Driving Licence

### Module 4 - Spreadsheets

### using Excel 2003

Release ECDL246v2

v

Published by:

> CiA Training Ltd
> Business & Innovation Centre
> Sunderland Enterprise Park
> Sunderland  SR5 2TA
> United Kingdom

> Tel: +44 (0) 191 549 5002
> Fax: +44 (0) 191 549 9005

> E-mail: info@ciatraining.co.uk
> Web: www.ciatraining.co.uk

> **ISBN-13:  978 1 86005 672 7**

**The following information applies <u>only</u> to candidates in Ireland.**

Acknowledgements:

> The European Computer Driving Licence is operated in Ireland by ICS Skills, the training and certification body of the Irish Computer Society.
> Candidates using this courseware should register online with ICS Skills through an approved ECDL Test Centre. Without a valid registration, and the allocation of a unique ICS Skills ID number or SkillsCard, no ECDL tests can be taken and no certificate, or any other form of recognition, can be given to a candidate.

> Other ECDL Foundation Certification programmes offered by ICS Skills include Equalskills, ECDL Advanced, ECDL WebStarter, ECDL ImageMaker, EUCIP and Certified Training Professional.

> Contact:          ICS Skills
>                   Crescent Hall
>                   Mount Street Crescent
>                   Dublin 2
>                   Ireland

> Website:          www.ics.ie/skills

> Email:            skills@ics.ie

First published 2008

# Downloading the Data Files

The data associated with these exercises must be downloaded from our website. Go to: *www.ciatraining.co.uk/data*. Follow the on screen instructions to download the appropriate data files.

By default, the data files will be downloaded to **My Documents \ CIA DATA FILES \ ECDL \ 4 Spreadsheets**.

If you prefer, the data can be supplied on CD at an additional cost. Contact the Sales team at *info@ciatraining.co.uk*.

# Aims

To provide the student with an understanding of fundamental spreadsheet concepts, practical experience in spreadsheet design and implementation of the basic functions involved within spreadsheets.

# Objectives

After completing the guide the user will be able to:

- Work with spreadsheets and save them in different file formats

- Choose built in options, such as the Help function, within the application to enhance productivity

- Enter data into cells and use good practice in creating lists; select, sort, copy, move and delete data

- Edit rows and columns in a worksheet; copy, move, delete and appropriately rename worksheets

- Create mathematical and logical formulas using standard spreadsheet functions; use good practice in formula creation and be able to recognise error values in formulas

- Format numbers and text content in a spreadsheet

- Choose, create and format charts to communicate information meaningfully

- Adjust spreadsheet page settings and check and correct spreadsheet content before finally printing spreadsheets.

# Assessment of Knowledge

At the end of this guide is a section called the **Record of Achievement Matrix**. Before the guide is started it is recommended that the user complete the matrix to measure the level of current knowledge.

Tick boxes are provided for each feature. **1** is for no knowledge, **2** some knowledge and **3** is for competent.

After working through a section, complete the **Record of Achievement** matrix for that section and only when competent in all areas move on to the next section.

# Contents

**SECTION 1 GETTING STARTED** ........................................................................................... **8**

　1 - Starting Excel ............................................................................................................. 9

　2 - The Excel Screen ...................................................................................................... 10

　3 - Menus ......................................................................................................................... 12

　4 - Toolbars ..................................................................................................................... 13

　5 - The Worksheet Window ........................................................................................... 15

　6 - Moving Around .......................................................................................................... 16

　7 - Help ............................................................................................................................ 17

　8 - The Office Assistant .................................................................................................. 19

　9 - Preferences ................................................................................................................ 21

　10 - Closing Excel ........................................................................................................... 23

　11 - Revision .................................................................................................................... 24

　12 - Revision .................................................................................................................... 25

**SECTION 2 OPEN AND CLOSE WORKBOOKS** ............................................................... **26**

　13 - Opening a Workbook ............................................................................................... 27

　14 - Closing a Workbook ................................................................................................ 28

　15 - Using Scroll Bars ..................................................................................................... 29

　16 - Opening Multiple Workbooks ................................................................................. 30

　17 - Revision .................................................................................................................... 31

**SECTION 3 CREATING AND SAVING WORKBOOKS** ...................................................... **32**

　18 - Starting a New Workbook ....................................................................................... 33

　19 - Entering Labels ........................................................................................................ 34

　20 - Entering Numbers .................................................................................................... 35

　21 - Saving a New Workbook ......................................................................................... 36

　22 - Saving a Named Workbook ..................................................................................... 37

　23 - Saving in Different Formats .................................................................................... 38

　24 - Saving as a Template ............................................................................................... 39

　25 - Revision .................................................................................................................... 40

　26 - Revision .................................................................................................................... 41

**SECTION 4 FORMULAS** ..................................................................................................... **42**

　27 - Formulas ................................................................................................................... 43

　28 - Brackets .................................................................................................................... 44

　29 - AutoSum ................................................................................................................... 45

　30 - Checking for Errors ................................................................................................. 47

　31 - Revision .................................................................................................................... 49

　32 - Revision .................................................................................................................... 50

**SECTION 5 WORKBOOKS** ......................................................................................... **51**

33 - MULTIPLE WORKSHEETS ................................................................................ 52

34 - SWITCH BETWEEN OPEN WORKBOOKS ...................................................... 53

35 - RENAMING SHEETS ........................................................................................ 54

36 - COPYING AND MOVING SHEETS .................................................................. 55

37 - INSERTING AND DELETING SHEETS ............................................................ 57

38 - REVISION ......................................................................................................... 58

**SECTION 6 EDITING** ...................................................................................................... **59**

39 - EDITING CELLS ............................................................................................... 60

40 - DELETING CELL CONTENTS ......................................................................... 62

41 - USING UNDO AND REDO ............................................................................... 63

42 - RANGES ........................................................................................................... 64

43 - USING THE FILL HANDLE .............................................................................. 66

44 - COPYING CELLS ............................................................................................. 67

45 - MOVING CELLS ............................................................................................... 69

46 - COPYING & MOVING BETWEEN WORKBOOKS ........................................ 71

47 - FINDING SPECIFIC TEXT ............................................................................... 72

48 - REPLACING TEXT ........................................................................................... 73

49 - SORTING .......................................................................................................... 74

50 - REVISION ......................................................................................................... 75

51 - REVISION ......................................................................................................... 76

**SECTION 7 PRINTING** ................................................................................................... **77**

52 - PRINTING ......................................................................................................... 78

53 - PRINT PREVIEW .............................................................................................. 79

54 - PAGE SETUP .................................................................................................... 80

55 - MARGINS ......................................................................................................... 82

56 - PRINTING A SELECTION ................................................................................ 83

57 - HEADERS AND FOOTERS .............................................................................. 84

58 - PRINT TITLES .................................................................................................. 86

59 - PRINT OPTIONS .............................................................................................. 87

60 - DISPLAYING & PRINTING FORMULAS ....................................................... 88

61 - REVISION ......................................................................................................... 89

62 - REVISION ......................................................................................................... 90

**SECTION 8 FORMATTING** ........................................................................................... **91**

63 - FORMATTING ................................................................................................... 92

64 - BOLD, UNDERLINE & ITALIC ...................................................................... 93

65 - FONTS & FONT SIZE ....................................................................................... 94

66 - FORMAT NUMBER .......................................................................................... 95

67 - DATES .............................................................................................................. 97

68 - ALIGNMENT .................................................................................................... 98

**SECTION 8 FORMATTING** ............................................................................................**CONTINUED**

  69 - CHANGING COLUMN WIDTH................................................................... 100

  70 - CHANGING ROW HEIGHT ...................................................................... 101

  71 - INSERTING ROWS AND COLUMNS ......................................................... 102

  72 - DELETING ROWS AND COLUMNS .......................................................... 103

  73 - ADDING BORDERS ................................................................................. 104

  74 - ADDING COLOUR ................................................................................. 106

  75 - ROTATE TEXT ...................................................................................... 107

  76 - FREEZING PANES ................................................................................. 108

  77 - ZOOM ................................................................................................... 109

  78 - REVISION ............................................................................................ 110

  79 - REVISION ............................................................................................ 111

**SECTION 9 FUNCTIONS & ADDRESSING** ......................................................... **112**

  80 - FUNCTIONS ......................................................................................... 113

  81 - COUNT ................................................................................................ 114

  82 - AVERAGE AND ROUND ........................................................................ 115

  83 - MAXIMUM AND MINIMUM ................................................................... 116

  84 - IF ........................................................................................................ 117

  85 - RELATIVE ADDRESSING ...................................................................... 118

  86 - ABSOLUTE ADDRESSING ..................................................................... 119

  87 - REVISION ............................................................................................ 120

  88 - REVISION ............................................................................................ 121

**SECTION 10 CHARTS**............................................................................................ **122**

  89 - INTRODUCING CHARTS ....................................................................... 123

  90 - CREATING CHARTS ............................................................................. 124

  91 - EMBEDDED CHARTS ............................................................................ 126

  92 - CHART TYPES ...................................................................................... 127

  93 - COPY, MOVE & RESIZE CHARTS ......................................................... 128

  94 - FORMATTING CHARTS ........................................................................ 129

  95 - CHART OPTIONS ................................................................................. 130

  96 - PRINTING CHARTS .............................................................................. 132

  97 - REVISION ............................................................................................ 133

  98 - REVISION ............................................................................................ 134

**ANSWERS** ............................................................................................................ **135**

**GLOSSARY** .......................................................................................................... **137**

**INDEX** .................................................................................................................. **138**

**RECORD OF ACHIEVEMENT MATRIX** ................................................................. **140**

**OTHER PRODUCTS FROM CIA TRAINING LTD** .................................................... **144**

# Section 1
# Getting Started

## By the end of this Section you should be able to:

**Understand Spreadsheet Principles**

**Start a Spreadsheet Program**

**Recognise the Spreadsheet Screen Layout**

**Work with Menus and Toolbars**

**Use Help and the Office Assistant**

**Change Preferences**

**Close a Spreadsheet Program**

To gain an understanding of the above features, work through the **Driving Lessons** in this **Section**.

For each **Driving Lesson**, read the **Park and Read** instructions, without touching the keyboard, then work through the numbered steps of the **Manoeuvres** on the computer. Complete the **Revision Exercise(s)** at the end of the section to test your knowledge.

# Driving Lesson 1 - Starting Excel

## ▣ Park and Read

A spreadsheet package is a computer program created specifically to help in the processing of tabular information, usually numbers. The spreadsheet stores information in rows (across the screen) and columns (down the screen), forming a worksheet (the *Excel* term for a spreadsheet).

Spreadsheets are most commonly used to manipulate figures. They can be used for accounting, cash flows, budgeting, forecasts, etc. Any job that involves the use of numbers can be done on a spreadsheet.

The biggest advantage that a spreadsheet has over other methods of manipulating data is its ability to constantly update figures without the user having to do any calculations.  Once a spreadsheet is set up, its calculations will always be correct and any changes in data are automatically updated.

Spreadsheets can also take raw data and present it in an attractive way, with formatted tables and charts.

## Manoeuvres

1.   There are numerous ways to start *Excel* depending on how the computer has been set up. The following method is recommended for beginners. Starting the computer will automatically show the *Windows* **Desktop**.

     Click once on **start** to show the list of start options available. All *Windows* applications can be started from here.

2.   Move the mouse pointer to **All Programs**.

3.   Click on **Microsoft Office** and then | Microsoft Office Excel 2003 |.

4.   The spreadsheet program *Excel* starts.

5.   The **Office Assistant** may be displayed. Click on it with the right mouse button and select **Hide** to remove it from the screen. This will be explained in more detail later.

# Driving Lesson 2 - The Excel Screen

## ⊡ Park and Read

On starting, *Excel* displays a blank workbook, as below, named **Book1** as shown in the **Title Bar**. A **workbook** is a file that can contain many **worksheets** but has 3 by default.

## ☞ Manoeuvres

1.   The *Excel* screen will be similar to the diagram below. Check the captions and identify the parts on the screen. **Sheet1** is displayed.

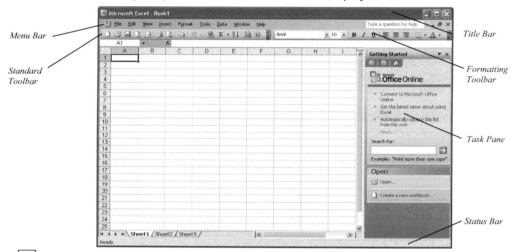

*Menu Bar*

*Standard Toolbar*

*Title Bar*

*Formatting Toolbar*

*Task Pane*

*Status Bar*

ℹ   *Some of the buttons may be different, because Excel automatically customises the **Toolbars** and **Menu** lists to reflect commonly selected options.*

2.   When certain options are selected in *Excel 2003* the program tries to download content from **Office Online**, by connecting to the Internet. This can become annoying, especially for users without an Internet connection, or with a slow, dial up connection. While working through this guide, disable the option. Select **Tools | Options**, make sure the **General** tab is selected and click **Service Options**. A new window will appear; select **Online Content** from the list on the left.

3.   If the **Show content and links from Office Online** box is checked, uncheck it and click **OK**. If it is not checked, just click **OK**. Click **OK** again to close the **Options** dialog box. This change will not take effect until *Excel* is restarted in a later Driving Lesson.

# Driving Lesson 2 - Continued

4.   The **Title Bar** is the top line of the *Excel* screen. It shows the application and the name of the workbook that is on the screen. Identify the **Title Bar**.

5.   The name of the current workbook is **Book1** or similar. Check this in the **Title Bar**.

6.   The second line is the **Menu Bar**, containing menus from **File** to **Help**. Check that there are nine menus.

7.   The next line is called the **Toolbar**. The left side is the **Standard Toolbar** and the right side the **Formatting Toolbar**. These have buttons to click to quickly select an action or basic feature. Move the cursor over any button but do not click. Read the **ToolTip**, which gives the name of that button.

8.   At the right of the screen is an area called the **Task Pane**, if this is not displayed, double click the **View** menu and then select **Task Pane** to display it.

9.   The **Task Pane** provides options for performing some common tasks. It appears, disappears and changes depending on the task currently being performed. On starting *Excel*, the first **Task Pane** deals with opening and creating various types of workbook. Look at the list of options available.

10.  To see the other available versions of **Task Panes**, click the down arrow at the right of the pane title bar.

11.  Click on **Clip Art** to display the **Task Pane** for that process.

12.  In the same way, look at each of the available **Task Panes**.

i   *The **Task Pane** can be hidden or displayed by using the **View | Task Pane** command. Having the **Task Pane** displayed is a personal preference of the user. This guide chooses not to have it displayed in order to see more of the worksheet.*

13.  To hide the **Task Pane**, select **View | Task Pane** or click the **Close** button at the right of the pane title bar.

14.  The **Status Bar** runs along the bottom of the window. This displays messages as tasks are performed. Check that the current message is **Ready**.

# Driving Lesson 3 - Menus

## ▣ Park and Read

The **Menu Bar** is displayed under the **Title Bar** and consists of drop down menus that contain commands to perform actions. The commands under each **Menu** name are personalised, unused items are hidden.

## ↱ Manoeuvres

1. Move the mouse pointer to the **Menu Bar**.

2. To open the **Edit** menu, position it directly over the menu name, **Edit**, and click once. A short list will appear as a drop down menu. This list of commands shows what actions can be carried out. Chevrons at the bottom indicate that not all options are visible. After a few seconds the list expands to show all the items. Double clicking **Edit** or clicking the chevrons, will display the full list immediately.

3. Some command names may appear as dim, pale, beige (ghosted) text. This indicates that these commands are not available for selection at the moment.

4. A picture alongside a command indicates that there is a button on a toolbar that will execute this command more easily.

5. Move to **View** on the **Menu Bar**. Ticks (✓) before command names are used to show which display options are in use.

6. Options with ▶ after the name lead to a sub menu so that further choices can be made. Place the mouse on **Toolbars** to display a sub menu.

7. On the **Menu Bar** move to **File**. Three dots after a command leads to a dialog box. Point to **Print** and click once to select that option.

8. Read the dialog box and click **Cancel** to close it.

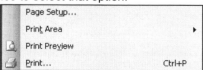

# Driving Lesson 4 - Toolbars

## ▣ Park and Read

Under the **Menu Bar** there are two toolbars, the left one is the **Standard Toolbar** and the right is the **Formatting Toolbar**.

     *Standard Toolbar*                    *Formatting Toolbar*

There are buttons on each of these toolbars that carry out specific tasks when they are clicked. To save space on the screen many buttons are hidden, but they are easily displayed. As buttons are used they replace others, which are then hidden.

## 🕭 Manoeuvres

1. The **Standard Toolbar** performs general tasks mainly from the **File** and **Edit** menus. Place the mouse pointer over the first button on the **Standard Toolbar** but do not click. *Excel* displays the **ToolTip New**.

2. Move the mouse pointer from button to button and read the **ToolTips**. These explain what each button is used for.

3. The **Formatting Toolbar** is to the right of the **Standard Toolbar**, by default. This is used for presentation, to make the spreadsheets easy to read by changing the way they look. Place the mouse pointer over the first button on the **Formatting Toolbar** but do not click. *Excel* displays the **ToolTip**.

4. Chevrons, 🗝 on a toolbar indicate that more buttons are available. Click the chevrons at the right of the **Standard Toolbar**. All the buttons not displayed for the **Standard** and **Formatting Toolbars** are shown. The buttons you can see will be different, because of the customisation.

# Driving Lesson 4 - Continued

5.  Click the chevrons again to hide the extra buttons.

6.  There are several **Toolbars** within *Excel* and they can be displayed or hidden. Select **View | Toolbars** to display the list.

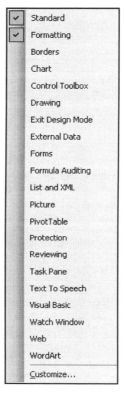

7.  Note that the **Standard** and **Formatting** toolbars are checked. The **Task Pane** is included here. Any items can be displayed or hidden by checking or un-checking from this list.

8.  Click on **Formatting** to hide it. Only the **Standard Toolbar** is displayed now.

9.  A quicker method to modify the toolbar display is to point at any toolbar and right click with the mouse. This displays a shortcut menu - the toolbar list from which any toolbar can be displayed or hidden. Right click on the **Standard Toolbar** and click on **Formatting** to display this toolbar again.

10. Use the **Shortcut Toolbar** menu again to make sure that the **Standard** and **Formatting** toolbars are the only toolbars displayed.

# Driving Lesson 5 - The Worksheet Window

## ▣ Park and Read

Spreadsheets help in the processing of numbers. They store information in **rows** (across the screen) and **columns** (down the screen). A **cell** is the intersection of a row and column. All the cells form a **worksheet** (the *Excel* term for a spreadsheet). Several **worksheets** are bound together and called a **workbook**.

## ⌒ Manoeuvres

1.  Move the mouse pointer to cell **B3** and click. The **Current** or **Active** cell is now **B3**. It has a dark border. Each cell is identified by the column letter and row number, which form the intersection, e.g. the cell formed where column **D** and row **8** meet is known as cell **D8**.

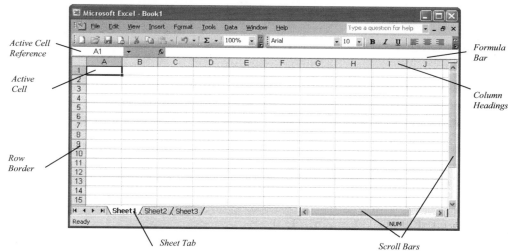

2.  Look for the **Active Cell Reference,** which is shown in the **Name Box** at the left of the **Formula Bar**. It displays **B3**.

3.  Click in cell **C6**. The **Active Cell Reference** now shows **C6**. These letters and numbers are shown highlighted in the **Row** and **Column Headings** on the worksheet. **C6** is now the **Current** or **Active cell**.

4.  The active cell can be moved using various key presses. Press the right cursor key →. The active cell moves right into cell **D6**.

5.  Press the down cursor ↓ to move into cell **D7**. Press the left cursor ← to move into **C7**.

6.  Press the up cursor ↑. The active cell should now be **C6** again.

# Driving Lesson 6 - Moving Around

## ▣ Park and Read

A worksheet is very large. The arrow keys are used for moving small distances. Other keys are used to move bigger distances.

## Manoeuvres

1.  Use the right cursor key → repeatedly to move to the column after **Z**. The alphabet is used again with **A** in front, i.e. **AA AB**, etc.

2.  The **<End>** key followed by an arrow key moves to the edge of the worksheet when empty. To move to the last column press **<End>** then the right arrow key →. The last column is **IV**.

3.  Press the **<Home>** key, this always returns the active cell to column **A** on the same row.

4.  Click on cell **D3**. Press **<End>** followed by the → key to move to **IV3**.

5.  Press the **<Home>** key to return to cell **A3**.

6.  Press **<End>** then the **Down** cursor key ↓. The active cell moves down to the last row, **65536**.

7.  Press **<Ctrl Home>** (hold down the **Control** key and press the **Home** key) to move back to cell **A1**. The key press **<Ctrl Home>** always moves the active cell back to **A1**.

8.  Click on a cell in the centre of the screen and press **<Ctrl Home>** to move to **A1**.

*There are other key presses and mouse actions that also move the active cell around a worksheet. These are covered later when a completed workbook is open.*

# Driving Lesson 7 - Help

## ▣ Park and Read

*Excel* has a comprehensive **Help** facility. This means that full advantage can be taken of the features incorporated in the program. Using **Help** can usually solve the majority of problems encountered.

## Manoeuvres

1.   Select **Help | Microsoft Excel Help** from the menu, or click the **Microsoft Excel Help** button, .

ℹ️ *If the **Office Assistant** appears, disable it by clicking the **Options** button (inside the speech bubble), uncheck **Use the Office Assistant** and click **OK**. Select **Help | Microsoft Excel Help** again.*

ℹ️ *To search for help topics using Office Online, the Online Content options must be switched on. To switch on Office Online select **Tools | Options**. Make sure the **General** tab is selected and click **Service Options**. A new window will appear. Select **Online Content** from the list on the left and check the **Show Content and Links from Office Online** and all of the check boxes below it. Click **OK** to make the changes. Click **OK** again to close the **Options** dialog box. This change will not take effect until Excel is restarted.*

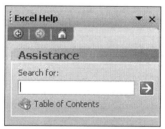

2.   **Help** can be searched for in two ways. Either type in keywords into the **Search for** box or search through the table of contents.

3.   Type **Insert** into the **Search for** box and click .

4.   The search results appear in the **Task Pane**. Select **Insert a Picture from a file** from the list. Notice that this shows the help in a new window.

5.   Read the help then close the window using the **Close** button, ⊠.

# Driving Lesson 7 - Continued

6.   Click the **Back** button, 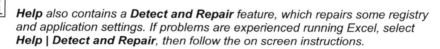, at the top of the **Task Pane**.

7.   Select **Table of Contents**, [⬥ Table of Contents]. Notice how the help topics are grouped into sections.

8.   Select **Working with Data** from the list, all topics associated with working with data will appear below and slightly indented from the main sections.

9.   Select **Entering Data** then **Entering and Editing Data** and then **Enter data in worksheet cells**, a new window will appear.

10.  In the new window select **Enter numbers, text, a date or a time** from the list of links.

11.  Read the **Help**.  Click the **Close** button, [✕], at the top right of the **Help** window to close it.

12.  Close the **Task Pane**.

[ℹ]  *Help also contains a Detect and Repair feature, which repairs some registry and application settings. If problems are experienced running Excel, select Help | Detect and Repair, then follow the on screen instructions.*

13.  Another feature is the **Type a Question for Help** box on the right of the **Menu Bar**, [date ▾] (this shows the most recent query used).

14.  Click the box and then type **how to print**. Press <**Enter**>. Select any topic from the results displayed in the **Task Pane** to obtain the required help.

15.  Close any open dialog boxes and close the **Task Pane**.

# Driving Lesson 8 - The Office Assistant

## 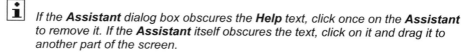 Park and Read

The **Office Assistant** is a way of providing instant help on tasks being undertaken. It consists of an animated character that displays a light bulb when it knows a quicker way of doing the task being undertaken or knows a handy tip.

## Manoeuvres

1.  Select **Help | Show the Office Assistant** to display the **Office Assistant**, which appears with a **What would you like to do?** dialog box.

2.  If the dialog box is not visible, click once on the **Assistant**. The dialog box will show data from any previous query or tips. The **Assistant** character may be different to the one shown above.

3.  Overtype the existing highlighted query text with **Format** and then click **Search**.

4.  A list of search results appears in the **Task Pane**. Scroll down to view all the search results.

5.  Move the mouse pointer over **Change formatting of text** until the cursor changes to 🖐. Click once to display the relevant **Help**.

ℹ️  *If the **Assistant** dialog box obscures the **Help** text, click once on the **Assistant** to remove it. If the **Assistant** itself obscures the text, click on it and drag it to another part of the screen.*

# Driving Lesson 8 - Continued

6.  Click on a topic. Read the **Help**.

7.  Click the **Close** button, ☒, at the top right of the **Help** window.

8.  Click again on the **Office Assistant** and type **AutoSum** in the **Search** text box.

9.  Click **Search** to view the results in the **Task Pane**.

10. Select **Add numbers** to display **Help**. Click on any topic to read it.

11. Return to the **Assistant** by closing the **Help** window and closing the **Task Pane**.

12. Right click on the **Office Assistant**.

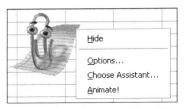

*The above **Assistant** shown is the default, **Clippit**.*

13. Select **Animate!** to see one of the character's animations. Repeat to see the various animated feats that **Office Assistant** can perform.

14. Right click on the **Office Assistant** and select **Hide** from the list to remove it. There may be a message offering the option of permanently turning off the **Office Assistant**, if so select **No, just hide me**.

> **i** *The **Assistant** can be displayed if hidden by selecting **Help | Show the Office Assistant**.*

> **i** *To disable the **Assistant**, display it, then click the **Options** button to display the **Office Assistant** dialog box. Within the **Options** tab, uncheck **Use the Office Assistant** and click **OK**.*

# Driving Lesson 9 - Preferences

## ▣ Park and Read

Basic options (**preferences**) can be changed in *Excel*, for example, the user name, which is added to certain templates. By default workbooks are opened from, and saved to the **My Documents** folder. These locations can also be changed.

## ↷ Manoeuvres

1.  Select **Tools | Options**. This dialog box sets and controls user preferences.

2.  The **View** tab is displayed by default, there are various options and check boxes, do not make any changes. Some of these settings are changed while working through this module.

3.  Display each tab in turn to see the available preferences.

4.  Select the **General** tab.

5.  To change the user details enter your own name in **User name**.

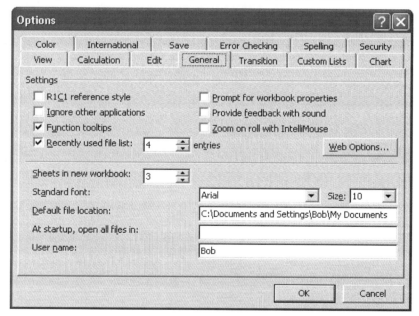

6.  Note that the **Default file location** is **My Documents**.

# Driving Lesson 9 - Continued

7.   This location can be changed to any folder on your computer, e.g. the working folder for this module is **My Documents\CIA DATA FILES\ECDL\4 Spreadsheets** and this could be entered in the **Default file location** box.

> *Setting the **Default file location** is a useful feature and will save time when opening and saving files. However, the location above could only be used temporarily while completing this guide. The setting would then need changing.*

8.   Click **OK**.

9.   Select **File | Properties** and the **Summary** tab.

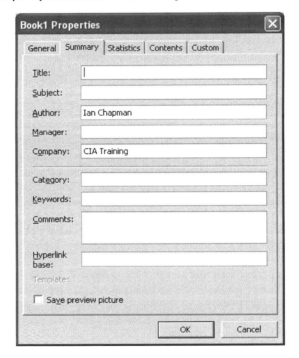

10.  Each workbook has a **Summary** attached. The author name is taken from **User name** in **Options**. The **Author** name shown is still the previous one. Your name will be displayed as the **Author** for every new workbook started from now.

11.  Click **Cancel**.

# Driving Lesson 10 - Closing Excel

## ▣ Park and Read

If any workbooks are still open when *Excel* is closed, a warning will be displayed with an option to save the changes.

## ♘ Manoeuvres

1. Double click the **File** menu to display the full drop down menu.

2. Place the mouse pointer over **Exit** at the bottom of the list and click once.

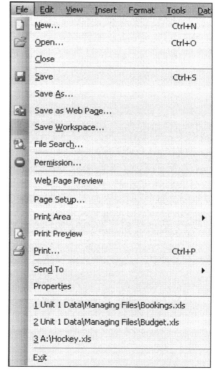

3. Select **No** if there is a prompt to save.

ℹ *Excel can also be closed by clicking the close button,* ☒ *in the top right corner of the screen or by pressing <Alt F4>.*

# Driving Lesson 11 - Revision

This Driving Lesson covers the features introduced in this section. Try not to refer to the preceding Driving Lessons while completing it.

1.   Start *Excel* using the **Start** button.

2.   How is the **Active Cell** displayed?

3.   How many worksheets are in a workbook by default?

4.   Use the mouse pointer to find **ToolTips** for the following buttons:

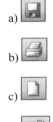

5.   How many options are listed within the **Edit Menu**, including those that are ghosted?

6.   How many options are **ghosted**?

7.   Use the **Help** command to view the help **Task Pane** showing how to move around in a workbook (Tip: use the **Search** or the **Table of Contents option**).

*Answers to this revision exercise can be found at the end of this guide.*

If you experienced any difficulty completing this Revision refer back to the Driving Lessons in this section. Then redo the Revision.

# Driving Lesson 12 - Revision

This Driving Lesson covers the features introduced in this section. Try not to refer to the preceding Driving Lessons while completing it.

1.  Display the **WordArt** toolbar.

2.  With a key press move to column **IV**. What did you press?

3.  Move down to the last row, what is the row number?

4.  Return to cell **A1** with a key press. What did you press?

5.  Hide the **WordArt Toolbar**.

6.  Leave *Excel* open for the next section.

**i**  *Answers to this revision exercise can be found at the end of this guide.*

If you experienced any difficulty completing this Revision refer back to the Driving Lessons in this section. Then redo the Revision.

Once you are confident with the features, complete the Record of Achievement Matrix referring to the section at the end of the guide. Only when competent move on to the next Section.

# Section 2
# Open and Close
# Workbooks

## By the end of this Section you should be able to:

**Open a Workbook**

**Open Multiple Workbooks**

**Use Scroll Bars**

**Close a Workbook**

To gain an understanding of the above features, work through the **Driving Lessons** in this **Section**.

For each **Driving Lesson**, read the **Park and Read** instructions, without touching the keyboard, then work through the numbered steps of the **Manoeuvres** on the computer. Complete the **Revision Exercise(s)** at the end of the section to test your knowledge.

# Driving Lesson 13 - Opening a Workbook

## ▣ Park and Read

**Workbooks** saved to disk can be opened to use again.

## ↱ Manoeuvres

1. To open an existing workbook, select the **File | Open** command from the **Menu Bar**. This will display the **Open** dialog box. **My Documents** is the default location.

2. Make sure that the data files for this module have been downloaded (see **Downloading the Data Files** on page 3). The data by default is stored in the folder **My Documents\CIA DATA FILES\ECDL\4 Spreadsheets**.

3. **My Documents** is the default location. Double click on **CIA DATA FILES**, then **ECDL** and then **4 Spreadsheets** to display the data files used with this module. Change the **View** to **List** if necessary, using the **View** button, 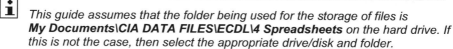.

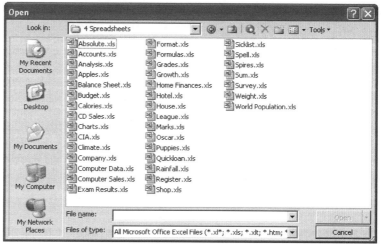

| ℹ️ | *This guide assumes that the folder being used for the storage of files is My Documents\CIA DATA FILES\ECDL\4 Spreadsheets on the hard drive. If this is not the case, then select the appropriate drive/disk and folder.* |
|---|---|

4. The *Excel* files will be displayed. *Excel* can also display files of other types if necessary by selecting from **Files of type** box.

5. In the list of files, click on **Hotel**, the workbook to be opened. Click the **Open** button.

| ℹ️ | *The file can also be opened by double clicking on its name in the list.* |
|---|---|

# Driving Lesson 14 - Closing a Workbook

## ▣ Park and Read

If a workbook is no longer to be used at this time, it needs to be closed.

## ⌒ Manoeuvres

1.  The workbook **Hotel** should still be on the screen from the previous Driving Lesson. If not, then open it.

2.  Select **File | Close** to close the workbook. If changes had been made to the workbook, the following dialog box would be displayed to prevent the accidental loss of the changes. In this instance, no changes have been made to the workbook, so it should close without displaying the dialog box (if the dialog box does appear, click on **No,** which will close without saving).

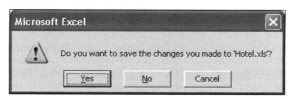

[i] *If closing a workbook created in an earlier version of Excel, a slightly different dialog box will be shown.*

[i] *The **Close Window** button can be used to close the workbook. Be careful not to close Excel. The key press <**Ctrl W**> can also be used to close the active window.*

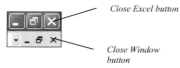

Close Excel button

Close Window button

3.  There should be no **Workbooks** open. If there are, select **File | Close** until the screen is different: the centre part is blank and most of the buttons are ghosted.

[i] *If a blank workbook is still displayed, close it, using **File | Close**.*

# Driving Lesson 15 - Using Scroll Bars

## P Park and Read

Small movements between adjacent cells are usually achieved using the cursor keys. However, when moving to a different area of the worksheet, the mouse and **Scroll Bars** are used.

## Manoeuvres

1.  Open the workbook **Spires** and click on cell **C3** to make it the **Active Cell**.

2.  The screen has a horizontal and vertical scroll bar, which can be used to scroll around the worksheet.

*Scroll Bar Arrows*

*Vertical Scroll Bar*

*Scroll Buttons*

*Horizontal Scroll Bar*

3.  Click the down arrow of the vertical scroll bar to move the worksheet down by one row. Continue to do this until row **6** is at the top of the screen. If you go too far this can be reversed by clicking on the up arrow.

4.  Click the right arrow of the horizontal scroll bar to move the worksheet right by one column. Continue to do this until column **D** is at the left of the screen.

5.  Notice that the **Active Cell Reference** field still reads **C3**. Even though it is not currently on the screen, **C3** is still the **Active Cell**.

6.  To move a whole screen view down, click once on the vertical scroll bar between the scroll button and the bottom arrow.

7.  To move a whole screen view right, click once on the horizontal scroll bar between the scroll button and the right arrow.

8.  Now click the vertical scroll button and drag it up. The work area scrolls continuously up until the mouse button is released.

9.  Now drag the horizontal scroll button to the left. The work area scrolls horizontally.

10. Now use the scroll buttons to view cell **A1**, then click on cell **B3** to make it the active cell.

11. Use the scroll buttons to scroll to the right and down as far as possible. Press **<Enter>** and the worksheet view will reset so that the new active cell, **B4**, is in the top left corner.

12. Leave the workbook **Spires** open.

# Driving Lesson 16 - Opening Multiple Workbooks

## Park and Read

More than one workbook can be open at the same time.

## Manoeuvres

1.  The workbook **Spires** should still be open, if not, open it.

2.  Open the workbook **Grades**.

3.  Both of these workbooks are now open. The **Taskbar** along the bottom of the screen shows each open workbook as a button.

> *If these two buttons are not on the **Taskbar**, select **Tools | Options | View** tab and check **Windows in Taskbar**. Click **OK**.*

> *There may be many other buttons on the **Taskbar** depending on the configuration of your computer and which other applications are running.*

4.  Notice how the button representing the workbook (**Grades**) being viewed appears to be pressed down.

5.  Click the **Spires** button to view that workbook. This workbook is now active.

6.  Open the workbook **Budget**. The **Taskbar** now shows three workbooks as buttons.

7.  Which workbook on the **Taskbar** appears to be pressed?

> *The key press <**Alt Tab**> can be used to switch from window to window.*

8.  Display **Spires**.

9.  Close all the open workbooks <u>without</u> saving.

> *Answers to this exercise can be found at the end of this guide.*

# Driving Lesson 17 - Revision

This is Driving Lesson covers the features introduced in this section. Try not to refer to the preceding Driving Lessons while completing it.

1.  Open the workbook **Hotel**. Maximise the window if necessary.

2.  Use the scroll bars to navigate to the edges of the blocks of occupied cells.

3.  Make **A1** the active cell in the **Hotel** workbook.

4.  Scroll down with the scroll button to display **Row 15** as the first row on the screen.

5.  Leave the **Hotel** workbook open and open the workbook **Grades**.

6.  Make **Hotel** the active workbook.

7.  Close the workbook **Hotel** <u>without</u> saving.

8.  Close the workbook **Grades** <u>without</u> saving.

If you experienced any difficulty completing this Revision refer back to the Driving Lessons in this section. Then redo the Revision.

Once you are confident with the features, complete the Record of Achievement Matrix referring to the section at the end of the guide. Only when competent move on to the next Section.

# Section 3
# Creating and Saving
# Workbooks

## By the end of this Section you should be able to:

**Start a New Workbook**

**Enter Text and Numbers**

**Save a New and Named Workbook**

**Save Workbooks in Different Formats**

**Save Workbook as a Template**

To gain an understanding of the above features, work through the **Driving Lessons** in this **Section**.

For each **Driving Lesson**, read the **Park and Read** instructions, without touching the keyboard, then work through the numbered steps of the **Manoeuvres** on the computer. Complete the **Revision Exercise(s)** at the end of the section to test your knowledge.

# Driving Lesson 18 - Starting a New Workbook

## ▣ Park and Read

A blank workbook based on the default template must be started to begin creating a new spreadsheet.

## ↱ Manoeuvres

1.  Start a new workbook by selecting **File | New**.

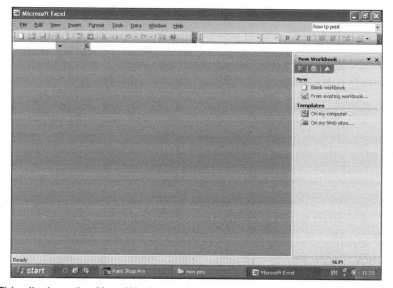

2.  This displays the **New Workbook Task Pane**. The main options are to start a new blank workbook based on the default template, create a new workbook based on an existing one, or create a new workbook based on a created template.

3.  Under the **New** heading, select **Blank Workbook** to create a new blank workbook.

4.  Close the current workbook using the **Close Window** button, ⊠.

5.  A new workbook can also be started with the **New** button. Click the **New** button, ⬚, on the **Standard Toolbar** to start a new workbook.

ℹ️ *This method starts a new workbook without displaying the **New Workbook Task Pane**.*

6.  Leave this blank workbook open for the next Driving Lesson.

# Driving Lesson 19 - Entering Labels

## ▣ Park and Read

**Labels** are normally used for describing the contents of the worksheet, as columns or row titles. When entering information into a cell, notice that the text appears in the **Formula Bar** as well as in the cell. A cell should really only ever contain one data item, e.g. a first name in one cell and a surname in an adjacent cell. This makes the data much easier to manipulate and sort. It's also good practice when creating a list of data to make sure it's easy to read. You can use a variety of layouts to do this: leave cells surrounding the list blank, leave a blank row before a row showing totals. Make sure you don't leave blank rows or columns in the main part of the list though.

## ⌒ Manoeuvres

1.  With a blank workbook on screen, click on cell **A3** to select it.

2.  Type the label **Fruit**. Notice **Enter** appears on the **Status Bar**, and that the **Enter** button appears in the **Formula Bar**. Press the <**Enter**> key to place the label into cell **A3**.

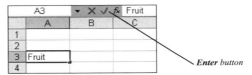

*Enter button*

ℹ️ *The entry can also be completed by clicking on the **Enter** box*

3.  Move to cell **B3** and type **Apples**. Place **Apples** in **B3** by pressing the right cursor key →. This automatically enters the data into **B3** and moves the active cell to the right, ready for the next entry.

ℹ️ *Selecting **Tools | Options | Edit** allows a choice of where the next entry will be placed after <**Enter**> is pressed. Found under **Move selection after Enter**, any direction may be selected. If listing labels along a row or down a column, use this to determine the direction after pressing <**Enter**>.*

4.  Select **Tools | Options | Edit** and check that **Move selection after Enter** is **Down**, then select **OK**. Complete the table by entering the data as opposite. If any mistakes are made, leave the errors.

| | A | B | C | D | E |
|---|---|---|---|---|---|
| 1 | | | | | |
| 2 | | | | | |
| 3 | Fruit | Apples | Pears | Oranges | Total |
| 4 | Jan | | | | |
| 5 | Feb | | | | |
| 6 | Mar | | | | |
| 7 | Total | | | | |
| 8 | | | | | |

5.  Leave the workbook open for the next Driving Lesson.

# Driving Lesson 20 - Entering Numbers

## ⊞ Park and Read

Numbers must begin with one of the following characters: **0 1 2 3 4 5 6 7 8 9 . + -** or a currency symbol.

## ⌇ Manoeuvres

1.  Use the workbook open from the previous Driving Lesson.

2.  Click on cell **B4** and type **36**, followed by **<Enter>**. The active cell is placed in cell **B5** ready for the next entry.

|   | A | B | C | D | E | F |
|---|---|---|---|---|---|---|
| 1 |   |   |   |   |   |   |
| 2 |   |   |   |   |   |   |
| 3 | Fruit | Apples | Pears | Oranges | Total |   |
| 4 | Jan | 36 | 38 | 26 |   |   |
| 5 | Feb | 40 | 26 | 37 |   |   |
| 6 | Mar | 53 | 20 | 41 |   |   |
| 7 | Total |   |   |   |   |   |
| 8 |   |   |   |   |   |   |

3.  Enter the rest of the above information into the correct cells, using the cursor movement keys to complete each entry.

**i** *Any instruction to enter or type information into a cell will assume that the entry is completed with a movement key, <**Enter**> key, clicking on another cell, etc.*

4.  Do **NOT** close the workbook as it is saved in a later Driving Lesson.

**i** *By default, all numeric values are right aligned (placed to the right edge of the column) and the labels (text) are left aligned. Alignment is dealt with in a later Driving Lesson.*

# Driving Lesson 21 - Saving a New Workbook

## Park and Read

After creating a worksheet, it needs to be saved as a workbook so it can be used again. The **Save** process includes selecting the location to save to, giving the workbook a name and selecting the type of format to save it in.

## Manoeuvres

1. With the worksheet open from the previous Driving Lesson, select the **Save** button, 🖫, or select **File | Save** from the menu or use the key press <**Ctrl S**>.

2. The **Save As** dialog box appears as this workbook has not been saved previously and no old version exists to overwrite.

3. In the **File name** box overtype to change the default workbook name to **Fruit**. The files for this guide are stored in the **4 Spreadsheets** folder, a sub folder **My Documents**, **CIA DATA FILES** and **ECDL**.

*After moving to the **4 Spreadsheets** folder earlier, Excel remains there until it is closed down or another location is selected. Excel, when restarted, will revert to the default folder, **My Documents**.*

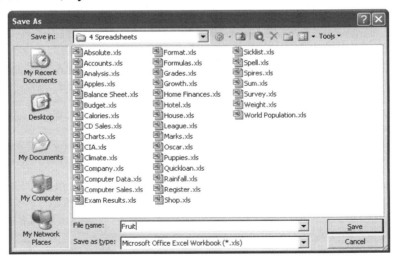

4. Click the **Save** button to save the file.

5. Check the **Title Bar** for the file name.

6. Leave the workbook **Fruit** open.

# Driving Lesson 22 - Saving a Named Workbook

## ▣ Park and Read

There are two commands used when saving a workbook.

**Save**          saves the file under the same name as previously used and overwrites an earlier version.

**Save As**       allows changes to be made to the initial save options creating a different version of the original, or to overwrite the original by confirming the replacement. This option can be used to create a backup of a file to a diskette (a floppy disk) or a memory stick.

## ⌐ Manoeuvres

1.    The workbook **Fruit** should still be on screen from the last Driving Lesson. Select cell **A1** and enter your name, then complete the entry.

2.    This workbook will now be saved as **Fruit2**. Select **File | Save As** to display the dialog box.

3.    Type or edit the name in the **File name** box to **Fruit2** to save the file with the new name. Check that the current folder is correct in the **Save in** box.

4.    Click on **Save**.

5.    This workbook has not changed but it can still be saved to overwrite the first copy. Select **File | Save As**, leave the filename as **Fruit2**, click the **Save** button to begin saving.

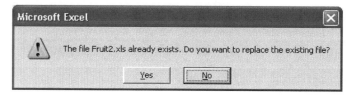

6.    Click **Yes** to replace the existing file. The workbook is saved.

7.    Close the workbook **Fruit2**.

8.    *Excel* can display the most recently opened workbooks at the bottom of the **File** menu. Open the workbook **Fruit** by selecting **File** and then clicking on **Fruit**. It should be exactly as saved earlier, i.e. without your name.

9.    Close the workbook **Fruit**.

# Driving Lesson 23 - Saving in Different Formats

## 🄿 Park and Read

Workbooks can be saved in a variety of formats: text, template, older versions of *Excel* and associated products.

## 🄿 Manoeuvres

1.  Open the workbook **Grades**.

2.  This workbook cannot be opened in older versions of *Excel* or other spreadsheet programs without being saved in the correct format. To save the workbook in a different format select **File | Save As**.

3.  In the **File name** box enter **Test Format**.

4.  Click the drop down arrow in the **Save as type** box.

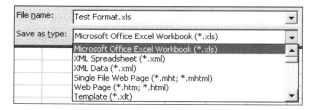

5.  Scan the list to display all the available formats that *Excel* can use. Choose the **Microsoft Excel 5.0/95 Workbook**, a previous version of *Excel*. Click **Save**.

6.  To save the file in another application's format select **File | Save As** and from the **Save as type** box, select **WKS (1-2-3)(*.wks)**. Change the file name to **Test2**. Click **Save**.

7.  If a workbook contains features that are not supported in the chosen format, an error message is displayed about losing formatting. This is a much simpler spreadsheet application; click **Yes** to lose some formatting. The workbook is saved as **Test2.wks**. This file can be opened in **Works**.

8.  To save the workbook as **Text**, select **File | Save As** and from the **Save as type** box, select **Text (Tab delimited) (*.txt)** and change the file name to **Test3**. Click **Save**. Select **Yes** at the prompt. The workbook is saved as **Test3.txt**. This text file can be opened in *Notepad*, *WordPad* or *Word*.

9.  Leave the workbook open.

# Driving Lesson 24 - Saving as a Template

## ▣ Park and Read

An *Excel* worksheet can be saved as a **template**, so that it can be used as a starting point from which to create new worksheets.

## ⌒ Manoeuvres

1.  Use the workbook **Grades**.

2.  To save the workbook as a template, select **File | Save As**. In the **Save As** dialog box, change the **File name** to **Scores** and from **Save as type** select **Template (*.xlt)**.

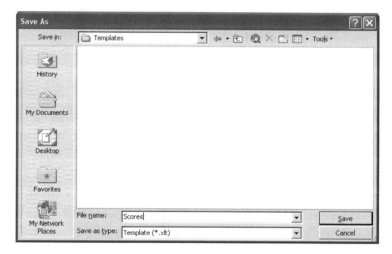

3.  Click **Save**.

ℹ️  *A **Template** is a base workbook that is stored with other templates. They have an **.xlt** extension and are shown with a ▦, icon. To use a template select **File | New** and from the **New Workbook** task pane click ▦ General Templates... . Available templates will be displayed in the **Templates** dialog box.*

4.  Close the workbook.

5.  Select to open a file. Navigate to the **4 Spreadsheets** folder, then click **Cancel**. This navigation is done now in preparation for later, as after saving to the **Templates** folder, the **Save to** location remains the same.

# Driving Lesson 25 - Revision

This Driving Lesson covers the features introduced in this section. Try not to refer to the preceding Driving Lessons while completing it.

1.    Start with a new workbook.

2.    Create the following worksheet in the columns and rows indicated.

|   | A | B | C | D | E | F |
|---|---|---|---|---|---|---|
| 1 | Fred Bloggs | | | | | |
| 2 | | | | | | |
| 3 | Number | Add | Subtract | Multiply | Divide | |
| 4 | First | 6 | 7 | 5 | 12 | |
| 5 | Second | 3 | 4 | 3 | 4 | |
| 6 | Result | | | | | |
| 7 | | | | | | |

3.    Save the workbook as **Maths** and close it.

4.    Start a new workbook.

5.    Create the following worksheet:

|   | A | B | C | D |
|---|---|---|---|---|
| 1 | Formatting Section | | | |
| 2 | | | | |
| 3 | Exercise | Title | | |
| 4 | 39 | General Formatting | | |
| 5 | 40 | Format Cells | | |
| 6 | 41 | Format Number | | |
| 7 | 42 | Date and Time | | |
| 8 | 43 | Alignment | | |
| 9 | 44 | Wrap Text | | |
| 10 | 45 | Merge Cells | | |
| 11 | 46 | Text Orientation | | |
| 12 | 47 | Borders | | |
| 13 | 48 | Revision | | |
| 14 | | | | |

6.    Save the workbook as **Formatting Section** and close it.

If you experienced any difficulty completing this Revision refer back to the Driving Lessons in this section. Then redo the Revision.

# Driving Lesson 26 - Revision

This Driving Lesson covers the features introduced in this section. Try not to refer to the preceding Driving Lessons while completing it.

1.     Start with a new workbook.

2.     Create the following worksheet in the columns and rows indicated.

| | A | B | C | D | E | F | G | H | I |
|---|---|---|---|---|---|---|---|---|---|
| 1 | Satellite Sales Figures | | | | | | | | |
| 2 | | | | | | | | | |
| 3 | | Mon | Tue | Wed | Thu | Fri | Sat | Sun | Total |
| 4 | Zara | 0 | 3 | 5 | 3 | 2 | 4 | 5 | |
| 5 | George | 4 | 5 | 3 | 0 | 7 | 6 | 2 | |
| 6 | Ishmael | 3 | 2 | 0 | 6 | 4 | 5 | 3 | |
| 7 | Liz | 3 | 6 | 2 | 4 | 5 | 10 | 0 | |
| 8 | Total | | | | | | | | |

3.     Save the workbook as **Satellite**.

4.     Save the workbook as **Satellite4** in a worksheet format that can be opened in **Excel 4.0**. As *Excel 4.0* does not support multiple worksheets, a message box is displayed, click **OK** to save the active worksheet.

5.     Close the workbook **Satellite4**.

6.     Open the workbook **Quickloan**.

7.     Save the worksheet as a **template**, as **Loan**.

8.     Close the workbook.

9.     Open the workbook **Calories**.

10.    Enter your name in cell **A3**.

11.    Test the calories counter, using your own details.

12.    Save the workbook as a **template**, named **Calorie Intake**.

13.    Close the workbook.

If you experienced any difficulty completing this Revision refer back to the Driving Lessons in this section. Then redo the Revision.

Once you are confident with the features, complete the Record of Achievement Matrix referring to the section at the end of the guide. Only when competent move on to the next Section.

# Section 4
# Formulas

## By the end of this Section you should be able to:

**Enter Basic Formulas**

**Use AutoSum**

**Check Formulas**

**Check Spelling**

To gain an understanding of the above features, work through the **Driving Lessons** in this **Section**.

For each **Driving Lesson**, read the **Park and Read** instructions, without touching the keyboard, then work through the numbered steps of the **Manoeuvres** on the computer. Complete the **Revision Exercise(s)** at the end of the section to test your knowledge.

# Driving Lesson 27 - Formulas

## ▣ Park and Read

A calculation in *Excel* is called a **Formula**. All formulas begin with an equals =
sign, followed by the calculation. The calculation consists of cell references or
numbers separated by a mathematical symbol (+ add, - subtract, * multiply, /
divide), e.g. **=A1+A2**

Formulas are used to calculate answers from numbers that are entered on to a
sheet. To create formulas properly you should enter the cell references of those
cells used in the calculation, rather than just typing in the numbers. This means
that if the numbers in these cells are changed later, the formulas will be
recalculated and will still be correct.

## ⌁ Manoeuvres

1.  Start a new workbook, move the cell pointer to **B2** and type in **66**. Move to
    cell **B3** and type **34**.

2.  Move to cell **B4** and enter the formula to add the contents of cells **B2** and
    **B3** by typing in **=B2+B3 <Enter>**. Click in cell **B4** and note the cell display
    of **100** and the formula in the **Formula Bar**.

| B4 | ▼ | $f_x$ =B2+B3 | |
|---|---|---|---|
| | A | B | C | D |
| 1 | | | | |
| 2 | | 66 | | |
| 3 | | 34 | | |
| 4 | | 100 | | |
| 5 | | | | |

3.  In **B6** type in this formula, which divides B2 by B3: **=B2/B3**. The answer
    is **1.941176**.

4.  Move to cell **A8** and enter the following numbers (use the right directional
    arrow to complete each entry) into these cells:

    **A8 35, B8 23, C8 56, D8 99, E8 55**.

5.  Move to cell **F8** and type in this formula **=A8+B8+C8+D8+E8 <Enter>**.
    The answer should be **268**.

6.  Move back to cell **F8** and enter an = sign to begin the formula. Select cell
    **A8**, it appears in the **Formula Bar**. Type in the **+** symbol, then select cell
    **B8** and continue entering the **+** symbol and selecting the other cells until
    the formula is complete. Press **<Enter>**.

7.  Move to cell **B8** and change the value to **43** by over-typing the original
    value. Press **<Enter>** and the formula in cell **F8** is instantly recalculated. A
    spreadsheet containing formulas is never out of date.

8.  Leave the workbook open for the next Driving Lesson.

# Driving Lesson 28 - Brackets

## ▣ Park and Read

When more than one symbol is used in a formula, then the order becomes important, e.g. **A1+A2/A3**. *Excel* performs calculations in this order: **B**rackets over **D**ivision, **M**ultiplication, **A**ddition and finally **S**ubtraction (the **BODMAS** theory).

## ⤴ Manoeuvres

1. Click the **Sheet2** tab at the bottom left of the screen (there is more than one worksheet in each workbook, clicking on a **Sheet** tab displays that sheet) and create the following small worksheet.

   |   | A | B | C |
   |---|---|---|---|
   | 1 |   |   |   |
   | 2 | Sell Price | 10 |   |
   | 3 | Buy Price | 6 |   |
   | 4 | Sold | 4 |   |
   | 5 | Profit |   |   |
   | 6 |   |   |   |

2. To calculate the profit, click on cell **B5** and type the formula **=B2-B3*B4** and press <**Enter**> to complete the formula.

3. The answer is given as **-14**, this is because multiplication is carried out before the subtraction, according to the **BODMAS** theory.

4. Click on cell **B5** and re-enter the formula, this time add the brackets around the subtraction part of the formula, as below, the old formula is replaced by the new.

   | B5 | ▼ | *fx* =(B2-B3)*B4 | |
   |---|---|---|---|
   | | A | B | C | D |
   | 1 | | | | |
   | 2 | Sell Price | 10 | | |
   | 3 | Buy Price | 6 | | |
   | 4 | Sold | 4 | | |
   | 5 | Profit | 16 | | |
   | 6 | | | | |

5. Check the answer displayed. Profit per item **10-6**, which is **4**, multiplied by the number sold, **4**, giving **16**.

6. Close the workbook <u>without</u> saving the changes.

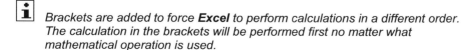

*Brackets are added to force **Excel** to perform calculations in a different order. The calculation in the brackets will be performed first no matter what mathematical operation is used.*

# Driving Lesson 29 - AutoSum

## ▣ Park and Read

The most common mathematical operation is addition. This calculation has been simplified by the use of a **Function** called **AutoSum**, Σ ▾ , on the **Standard Toolbar**. **AutoSum** adds the contents of cells automatically.

## ⌁ Manoeuvres

1.  Start a new workbook.

2.  In the following cells, enter the following numbers:

| | A | B | C | D | E |
|---|---|---|---|---|---|
| 1 | | | | | |
| 2 | | 2 | 1 | 3 | |
| 3 | | 3 | 5 | 2 | |
| 4 | | 4 | 2 | 1 | |
| 5 | | | | | |

3.  Click in cell **B5** and click the **AutoSum** button, Σ ▾ , on the **Standard Toolbar**.

| | A | B | C | D | E |
|---|---|---|---|---|---|
| 1 | | | | | |
| 2 | | 2 | 1 | 3 | |
| 3 | | 3 | 5 | 2 | |
| 4 | | 4 | 2 | 1 | |
| 5 | | =SUM(B2:B4) | | | |
| 6 | | SUM(**number1**, [number2], …) | | | |
| 7 | | | | | |

4.  Press <**Enter**> to complete the entry. The answer should be **9**.

5.  Repeat this in cells **C5** and **D5**.

6.  **AutoSum** also adds cells across. Click on cell **E2** and click the **AutoSum** button. Press <**Enter**> to complete the entry.

7.  Close the workbook <u>without</u> saving.

8.  Open the workbook **Sum**.

9.  Select cell **B7**. The three numbers above need to be added together to find the number of apples sold in the three month period.

# Driving Lesson 29 - Continued

10.  Click the **AutoSum** button, Σ ▾

| | A | B | C | D | E |
|---|---|---|---|---|---|
| 1 | | | | | |
| 2 | | | | | |
| 3 | Fruit | Apples | Pears | Oranges | Total |
| 4 | Jan | 36 | 38 | 26 | |
| 5 | Feb | 40 | 26 | 37 | |
| 6 | Mar | 53 | 20 | 41 | |
| 7 | Total | =SUM(B4:B6) | | | |
| 8 | | SUM(**number1**, [number2], ...) | | | |
| 9 | | | | | |

11.  Finish the formula by pressing **<Enter>** to sum the numbers above. The answer should be **129**.

12.  Move to cell **E4** and click the **AutoSum** button, Σ ▾. The January figures are selected, press **<Enter>** to complete the formula. The answer should be **100**.

ℹ️  *AutoSum adds the cells above or left depending on where the figures are located. If **AutoSum** has figures in both directions it will sum the cells above by default, if no other formulas are involved.*

13.  Use **AutoSum** to calculate the totals for the rest of the worksheet, even **E7** the grand total (adding cells to the left or above displays the same result).

ℹ️  *Be careful with cell **E6**. After clicking Σ ▾ you will need to click with the mouse and drag to select the cells from **B6** to **D6**, as the cells above **E6** are selected by default.*

14.  Save the workbook as **Sum Complete** and close it.

# Driving Lesson 30 - Checking for Errors

## ▣ Park and Read

A worksheet is of little use if one formula within it is incorrect or a cell contains a typing or spelling error. It is important that workbooks that are to be distributed are checked so that the worksheets contain no text or formula errors.

Formulas must be checked to see that they refer to the correct cells. Some formulas produce #**MESSAGE** denoting an error. Types of errors you need to recognise are:

| | |
|---|---|
| **#DIV/0!** | Division by zero |
| **#REF!** | Cell referenced is not valid |
| **#NAME?** | Does not recognise text in a formula |

You may also come across the following errors:

| | |
|---|---|
| **#NULL!** | The two areas specified do not intersect |
| **#VALUE!** | The wrong argument used |
| **#NUM!** | Error with number in formula |
| **#N/A** | The value used in the formula is not available |
| **######** | The result is too long to fit into the cell |

Typing and spelling mistakes can be checked either visually, or better still using *Excel's* spell checking facility. Corrections can then be made as appropriate.

## ⌫ Manoeuvres

1. Start a new workbook.

2. In cell **B3** type **6**, in cell **D3** type **8**, in cell **B5** type **10** and in cell **D5** enter the formula **=B3+B5-D3**. Press **<Enter>**.

3. Double click on cell **D5** to check the formula.

| | A | B | C | D | E |
|---|---|---|---|---|---|
| 1 | | | | | |
| 2 | | | | | |
| 3 | | 6 | | 8 | |
| 4 | | | | | |
| 5 | | 10 | | =B3+B5-D3 | |
| 6 | | | | | |

**ⓘ**    *Excel uses a different colour for each part of the formula.*

4. If your screen matches the above diagram then it is correct. Press **<Enter>**.

5. Close the workbook <u>without</u> saving.

# Driving Lesson 30 - Continued

6.  Open the workbook **Formulas**. Check the formulas on row **6** and cell **B12** for errors by double clicking on each cell. Remember to press <**Esc**> to cancel after checking.

7.  There is an error in cell **D6**, it contains a value, not a formula. Enter a formula in cell **D6** to multiply the two numbers above (**=D4\*D5**).

8.  Click on cell **E5** and enter **0**. The cell **E6** displays the **#DIV/0!** error message, division by zero.

9.  Close the workbook <u>without</u> saving.

10. Open the workbook **Spell**.

11. With **A1** the active cell, click the **Spelling** button, 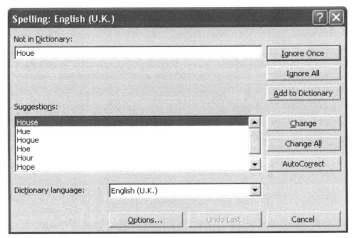, or select **Tools | Spelling**.

12. The **Spelling** dialog box will show the first mistake. **A1** is highlighted. The cell should read **House**. The **Suggestions** box displays **House**, click the **Change** button to correct the error.

13. The **Spelling** dialog box finds the next mistake in cell **A4**. The cell should read **Other**, the **h** has been missed out. Click on **Other** in the **Suggestions** list and click the **Change** button. Correct the other mistakes on the worksheet.

**i**   *Text can directly be entered into the **Change to** box if the required word is not in the **Suggestions** list or the error can be ignored.*

14. When finished spell checking, select **OK**.

15. Close the workbook <u>without</u> saving.

# Driving Lesson 31 - Revision

This Driving Lesson covers the features introduced in this section. Try not to refer to the preceding Driving Lessons while completing it.

1.    On a blank worksheet enter the numbers in the cells to match below.

|    | A | B | C | D | E | F |
|----|---|---|---|---|---|---|
| 1  |   |   |   |   | 4 |   |
| 2  |   |   |   |   | 7 |   |
| 3  |   |   |   |   | 5 |   |
| 4  |   |   |   |   | 2 |   |
| 5  |   |   |   |   | 4 |   |
| 6  |   |   |   |   | 3 |   |
| 7  |   |   |   |   | 8 |   |
| 8  |   |   |   |   | 9 |   |
| 9  | 8 | 2 | 4 | 7 |   |   |
| 10 |   |   |   |   |   |   |

2.    Click in cell **E9**. **AutoSum** is to be used. Will it sum the column or the row?

3.    Click the **AutoSum** button. Press **<Enter>**. What is the answer?

4.    Delete the answer in cell **E9** by clicking in cell **E9** and pressing the **<Delete>** key. You now need to sum the row of numbers. Click the **AutoSum** button, then click and drag from **A9** to **D9** or **D9** to **A9**. Press **<Enter>** to complete the formula. What is the answer?

5.    Click on cell **E3** and delete the contents.

6.    Delete the answer in **E9**.

7.    With cell **E9** active click the **AutoSum** button. You need to add all the column, click and drag the range **E1:E8**, press **<Enter>**. What is the answer?

8.    Close the workbook <u>without</u> saving it.

**i**   *Answers to this revision exercise can be found at the end of this guide.*

If you experienced any difficulty completing this Revision refer back to the Driving Lessons in this section. Then redo the Revision.

# Driving Lesson 32 - Revision

This Driving Lesson covers the features introduced in this section. Try not to refer to the preceding Driving Lessons while completing it.

1.  Start a new workbook. The worksheet below contains data on boxes of fruit. Insert the following information in the cells indicated.

| | A | B | C | D | E |
|---|---|---|---|---|---|
| 1 | Fruit Sales | | | | |
| 2 | | | | | |
| 3 | Fruit | Apples | Pears | Oranges | Total |
| 4 | Jan | 6 | 8 | 12 | |
| 5 | Feb | 7 | 6 | 10 | |
| 6 | Mar | 11 | 5 | 9 | |
| 7 | Total | | | | |
| 8 | Sell Price | | | | |
| 9 | Income | | | | |
| 10 | Buy Price | | | | |
| 11 | Profit | | | | |
| 12 | | | | | |

2.  Use **AutoSum** to sum the sales for each fruit (in **Row 7**) and for each month (in **Column E**). Calculate a grand total in cell **E7** (using either the column totals to the left or the row totals above).

3.  The selling prices of the three fruits are **9**, **11** and **13** for the apples, pears and oranges respectively. Enter this information.

4.  The **Income** row contains formulas that multiply the **Total** by the **Sell Price**. Complete the three cells.

5.  The buying prices of the three fruits are **5**, **6** and **7** for the apples, pears and oranges respectively. Enter this information.

6.  The **Profit** is a more complicated formula, containing brackets. Work out the profit for one box of fruit using subtraction in brackets and multiply by the total number of boxes sold. The result in cell **B11** should be **96**.

7.  Create similar formulas to calculate the profit for the pears and oranges.

8.  Use **AutoSum** to calculate the total income in cell **E9** and total profit in cell **E11**. This should be **377**.

9.  Check all the formulas by double clicking on each in turn and then save the completed workbook as **Fruit Sales** and close it.

If you experienced any difficulty completing this Revision refer back to the Driving Lessons in this section. Then redo the Revision.

Once you are confident with the features, complete the Record of Achievement Matrix referring to the section at the end of the guide. Only when competent move on to the next Section.

# Section 5
# Workbooks

## By the end of this Section you should be able to:

**Use Multiple Worksheets, Workbooks**

**Switch Between Open Workbooks**

**Rename Worksheets**

**Copy and Move Between Worksheets, Workbooks**

**Insert and Delete Worksheets**

To gain an understanding of the above features, work through the **Driving Lessons** in this **Section**.

For each **Driving Lesson**, read the **Park and Read** instructions, without touching the keyboard, then work through the numbered steps of the **Manoeuvres** on the computer. Complete the **Revision Exercise(s)** at the end of the section to test your knowledge.

# Driving Lesson 33 - Multiple Worksheets

## ▣ Park and Read

A workbook can contain up to 255 different worksheets, each with a different name. This allows related information to be kept together in the same workbook and complicated spreadsheet models to be created.

More than one workbook can open at the same time. This allows data, sheets and other objects to be copied or moved between workbooks.

## ⟲ Manoeuvres

1.  Open the workbook **CIA**. This is a workbook containing **16** worksheets, representing a company with sixteen area divisions around the country.

2.  Notice the sheet tabs across the bottom of the screen. Click on tab **Sheet3**. This makes the sheet active. All the 16 sheets are not displayed because of the amount of space.

*First    Left   Right   Last*

3.  There are 4 buttons to the left of **Sheet1** that control the sheet display. Click the **Last Sheet** button to switch to **Sheet16**. Click the sheet tab to make it active, the division name is in cell **B9**.

4.  Move the divider between the tabs and the scroll bar to give more space to show more tabs.

*Move pointer until ┿┝ appears and drag until*
*the required distance is achieved*

5.  Practise using the sheet display buttons to view all the sheets.

6.  Leave the workbook open for the next Driving Lesson.

 *To adjust the number of sheets in a default workbook from 3. Select **Tools | Options**, **General** tab and change the value in the **Sheets in new workbook** box. Click **OK**.*

# Driving Lesson 34 - Switch Between Open Workbooks

## ⊞ Park and Read

More than one workbook can be open at the same time. When a workbook is opened, it is displayed in the active window. Any previously opened workbooks are still open, but are hidden and not active.

## ⌐ Manoeuvres

1.   The **CIA** workbook should still be open. If not, open it. Open the workbook **Computer Sales**.

2.   Remember each workbook is displayed with its own button on the **Taskbar**. The active book has its button highlighted.

3.   Click on **CIA** to make it active.

**i**   *An alternative method to display a workbook is to select **Window** on the **Menu Bar**. The open books are numbered and listed at the bottom of the menu (the active book has a tick next to it). Selecting a name displays it.*

4.   Open the workbook **Climate** and then open **Company**.

5.   To display all open workbooks, double click the **Window** menu and select **Arrange**.

6.   **Tiled** is the default, click **OK** to display all open books tiled. The four books are displayed. Use the same command to display each arrangement in turn.

**i**   *Cascade is now rarely used, as the **Taskbar** is more effective for switching.*

7.   To display a single book, click the **Maximize** button of its window. Maximise **Climate**.

8.   Close **Climate**, then **Company**, then **Computer Sales**. Leave the **CIA** workbook open for the next Driving Lesson.

# Driving Lesson 35 - Renaming Sheets

## ▣ Park and Read

The names **Sheet1**, **Sheet2**, etc. are not very helpful for finding information. It makes much more sense to use meaningful names, which give a good idea of the content of the worksheet. The sheet tabs can contain up to **31** characters including spaces. Duplicate names are not allowed.

## ↱ Manoeuvres

1.  The workbook **CIA** should still be open. If not, open it.

2.  To rename **Sheet1** as **North**, double click the **Sheet1** tab, the name **Sheet1** is highlighted.

3.  Type the new name **North**.

4.  Either press <**Enter**> or click on any cell on the sheet.

ℹ️ *An alternative method is to use the menu command* ***Format | Sheet | Rename***.

5.  Rename **Sheet2** as **North East**.

6.  Rename all the other sheets with the name of the **Division** in cell **B9**, using any method.

7.  Save the workbook as **Divisions**.

8.  Leave the workbook open for the next Driving Lesson.

# Driving Lesson 36 - Copying and Moving Sheets

## Park and Read

Sheets within a workbook can be moved or copied within the same, or to a different workbook.

## Manoeuvres

1.   The workbook **Divisions** should still be open. If not, open it.

2.   Sheets can be moved and copied within the same workbook by dragging the sheet tab with the mouse. Move the **North Midlands** sheet between **South Wales** and **Midlands** by clicking and dragging to the correct position (a black triangle shows where the sheet will be inserted).

*Use the Sheet scroll buttons to locate the sheets that are not visible.*

3.   Move the **North West** sheet to between **North** and **North East**.

4.   A sheet is copied within the same workbook by holding <**Ctrl**> while dragging the sheet tab. Make a copy of the **North** sheet. Click and drag the **North** sheet tab while holding <**Ctrl**> across to the right, next to **North**. Release the mouse button first before <**Ctrl**>.

*The name of the copied sheet is **North (2)**. Duplicate sheet names are not allowed.*

5.   If a sheet is to be moved or copied to another workbook the shortcut menu is used. Right click the **North (2)** sheet tab.

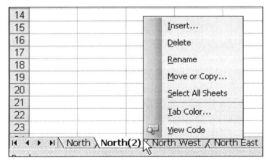

6.   This menu controls all the actions relating to sheets. Select **Move or Copy**.

# Driving Lesson 36 - Continued

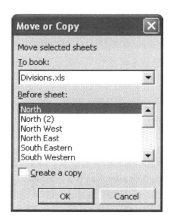

7.    To create a copy the **Create a copy** box is checked, otherwise the sheet is moved. Check the **Create a copy** box.

8.    To move or copy to a different workbook, a selection is made from the **To book** box. Drop down the list to see the available open workbooks A new workbook is to be created to contain the copied sheet. Select **(new book)**.

  *To move or copy to an existing workbook it must be open, so it is displayed in the **To book** box.*

9.    The **Before sheet** box is empty for a new workbook. An existing one would display all the sheets for a selection to be made on the placement. Click **OK**.

10.   A new workbook is created with just the sheet **North (2)** in it. Click **Divisions** on the **Taskbar** and check that **North (2)** is still in this book and that it was copied.

11.   Leave both workbooks open for the next Driving Lesson.

# Driving Lesson 37 - Inserting and Deleting Sheets

## 🅿 Park and Read

Once a workbook is open, sheets can be inserted or deleted to suit. The maximum number of sheets in a workbook is limited only by available memory.

## 👉 Manoeuvres

1.  Two workbooks, a new **Book** and **Divisions** are open from the previous Driving Lesson. The **South** division is to be closed because it is making vast losses. Right click the **South** tab in the **Divisions** workbook and select **Delete** from the shortcut menu.

2.  Click **Delete** to complete the deletion.

ℹ️ *An alternative method is to use **Edit | Delete Sheet** and confirm with **OK**.*

3.  The **Midlands** division is also doing poorly. Make **Midlands** active and delete it.

4.  Sheets are inserted before the active sheet. A new division called **Western** is to be created and it is to be located before the **Eastern** division. Right click on **Eastern** and select **Insert**. The **Worksheet** icon is selected, click **OK** to insert the sheet before **Eastern**.

ℹ️ *To insert a new worksheet the command **Insert | Worksheet** can be used.*

5.  Creating a new sheet similar to all the others will take too long. **Delete** the new sheet.

6.  Make **Eastern** active and create a copy. The new sheet is named **Eastern (2)**. Rename the sheet and cell **B9** to **Western**.

7.  Save the workbook **Divisions** using the same name and then close it.

8.  Close the unsaved workbook <u>without</u> saving.

# Driving Lesson 38 - Revision

This Driving Lesson covers the features introduced in this section. Try not to refer to the preceding Driving Lessons while completing it.

1.　　Open the workbook **Computer Sales**.

2.　　Delete the **Sales** sheet.

3.　　Copy the **Fruit** sheet to a new workbook.

4.　　Save the new workbook as **Copy** and then close it.

5.　　Insert a new sheet in **Computer Sales** ready to add more detailed information.

6.　　Rename the new sheet **Accounts**.

7.　　Display the **Fruit** sheet.

8.　　Save the workbook as **Computer Sales2**.

9.　　Close the workbook.

If you experienced any difficulty completing this Revision refer back to the Driving Lessons in this section. Then redo the Revision.

Once you are confident with the features, complete the Record of Achievement Matrix referring to the section at the end of the guide. Only when competent move on to the next.

# Section 6
# Editing

## By the end of this Section you should be able to:

**Edit Data in the Formula Bar and Cells**

**Delete Cell Contents**

**Use Undo and Redo**

**Select Ranges of Data**

**Use the Fill Handle**

**Erase and Sort Data**

**Cut, Copy and Paste**

**Find and Replace Text**

To gain an understanding of the above features, work through the **Driving Lessons** in this **Section**.

For each **Driving Lesson**, read the **Park and Read** instructions, without touching the keyboard, then work through the numbered steps of the **Manoeuvres** on the computer. Complete the **Revision Exercise(s)** at the end of the section to test your knowledge.

# Driving Lesson 39 - Editing Cells

## ◪ Park and Read

Changes can be made to data in cells in a variety of ways. The easiest way is to overtype one entry with another. When a cell entry is long or complicated small changes are either made in the **Formula Bar** or in the cell itself.

## ⟲ Manoeuvres

1.   Open the workbook **CD Sales**.

2.   Click the cell to be changed, in this case **B5**, **Quarters**.

3.   Enter the new data label, **Months** to replace **Quarters**.

4.   Before <**Enter**> is pressed, click the **Cancel** button, ☒, on the **Formula Bar**. This action cancels the new input, leaving the originally entered data unchanged.

*Cancel Button*

5.   Click on cell **C8** and type in **Months**. This time press the **Escape** key <**Esc**>. This cancels the input and is quicker when typing. These methods to cancel are used when data is accidentally entered into the wrong cell. **C8** contains a formula to calculate the profit.

6.   Type **Months** into cell **B5** again and press <**Enter**> to complete the entry. The new information replaces the old.

# Driving Lesson 39 - Continued

7.    Move into cell **B7**. Observe the cell contents in the **Formula Bar**. Click in the **Formula Bar** and change **Turnover** to **Income** using the **Backspace** key <←> (above <**Enter**>, make sure you don't use the left cursor key) to delete the text and typing in **Income**. Press <**Enter**> to complete the change.

**i**    *When editing, the <**Enter**> key must be used to end the process.*

8.    In cell **B8** edit **Profit** to **Gross Profit**.

**i**    *The full label cannot be seen. Do not worry about this. Widening columns is covered in Driving Lesson 69.*

9.    Enter your first name in cell **A1** and complete the entry.

10.    Double click in cell **A1**. A cursor is placed inside the cell to allow editing of the cell contents within the cell. If the cursor is not at the end of your first name, press the <**End**> key. Add a space and then your surname, press <**Enter**> to complete the entry.

11.    Double click in cell **A1** to edit the contents. Click and drag to highlight your first name. Press the <**Delete**> key to remove it. Press <**Enter**> to leave just your surname in the cell.

12.    Close the workbook **CD Sales** without saving.

# Driving Lesson 40 - Deleting Cell Contents

## ▣ Park and Read

*Excel* allows the user to erase or delete data in many ways.  Cell contents are erased by selecting **Edit | Clear | Contents** or by using **<Delete>** on the keyboard.

## 〽 Manoeuvres

1.   On a blank worksheet enter a number into cell **B4**. With **B4** selected erase the contents by selecting **Edit | Clear | Contents**.

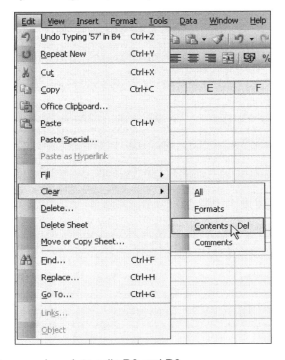

2.   Enter any two numbers into cells **B2** and **B3**.

3.   Select cell **B2** and then press **<Delete>**. The cell is now blank.

4.   Clear cell **B3**.

5.   Close the workbook <u>without</u> saving.

# Driving Lesson 41 - Using Undo and Redo

## 🅿 Park and Read

As it is so easy to remove the contents of a cell, *Excel* has **Undo** to reverse any mistakes that may have been made. After undoing the action, it can be redone, if necessary, using **Redo**.

## ↱ Manoeuvres

1. Open the workbook **CD Sales**.

2. Click in cell **E6** and press <**Delete**> to remove the cell contents.

3. Now delete the contents of cell **F6**.

4. Select **Edit | Undo Clear** to reverse the last action, i.e. put the contents back in **F6**.

🛈 *The exact wording after **Undo** is dependent on the action that has just been carried out.*

5. Now click the **Undo** button, 🔄, to replace the deletion before last.

6. After undoing an action, it can be redone by either selecting **Edit | Redo...** or clicking the **Redo** button, 🔁. Click the **Redo** button, 🔁, to reverse the last action, the **Undo**.

7. Use **Undo** to return the worksheet to its original state.

8. Delete the contents of cells **B5**, **C5**, **D5**, **E5** and **F5** one at a time. All actions that can be undone are stored in the **Undo** history.

9. To use this, click the drop down list next to the **Undo** button, 🔄.

10. Click the last **Clear** to **Undo 5 Actions** (there are a maximum of 16). The 5 deletions are restored.

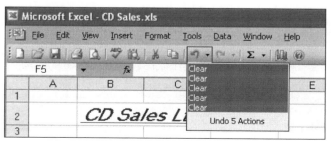

11. Close the workbook **CD Sales** <u>without</u> saving the changes.

# Driving Lesson 42 - Ranges

## ▣ Park and Read

A **range** is a rectangular selection of cells. Just as a single cell is identified by a cell reference, ranges are identified by the cells of their outer limits, e.g. the four cells B2, B3, C2 and C3 is the range **B2:C3**. Ranges are selected by clicking the mouse button and dragging to highlight a range of cells (known as **Click and Drag**).

Entire rows, columns, multiple rows, multiple columns and the entire worksheet can be selected using a similar technique.

Selections are made to allow the highlighted cells to be worked on, i.e. formatted, copied, moved, deleted, etc.

## ☞ Manoeuvres

1.  On a new worksheet click on cell **B2**. Click and drag down and to the right so that a range of six cells is highlighted, as shown below.

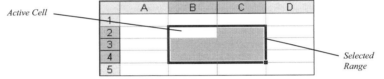

2.  Release the mouse button. Notice that the first cell in the range remains white and the other cells are highlighted.

3.  Selected ranges can be increased and decreased from the first cell in the range. Hold down the <**Shift**> key and select cell **E7**. The range is increased. Select cell **C2** while holding down <**Shift**> and the range is decreased.

4.  Click anywhere on the worksheet to remove the highlighted range.

5.  Select the range **B2:C4** again. Press and hold down the <**Ctrl**> key. Click and drag the range **C5:D6**. Release the <**Ctrl**> key. There should now be two separate ranges highlighted. Click anywhere on the sheet to remove the selected ranges.

6.  Click the **B** in the column border. Column **B** is now highlighted. Click on any cell to remove the selection.

7.  Click on **5** in the row border. Row **5** is now highlighted. Click on any cell to remove the selection.

8.  To select adjacent multiple columns, click in the column border and drag to select the required columns. Select columns **C** to **E**.

# Driving Lesson 42 - Continued

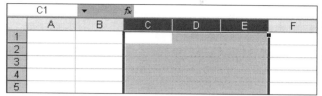

*These diagrams have been captured running Excel in Windows XP.*

9.  To select multiple adjacent rows, click and drag in the row border. Click and drag from **3** to **5**. Several rows are highlighted.

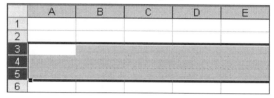

10. Click anywhere to remove the highlight.

11. Non adjacent rows or columns can be selected using the same technique as for ranges, i.e. hold down the **<Ctrl>** key to select the separate part. Select rows **2** to **5** and **8** to **10**.

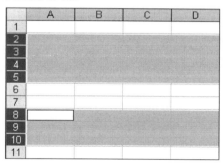

12. Select columns **B**, **C** and **E**.

13. To select the entire worksheet, click the **Select All** button (to the left of **A** and above **1**).

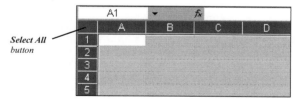

*Select All button*

14. Click on any cell to remove the highlighting.

# Driving Lesson 43 - Using the Fill Handle

## ▣ Park and Read

The **Fill Handle** quickly copies or increments data to a range of cells. If the data is in the form of days, dates, time, months or text with a number then the **Fill Handle** will increment as it fills, otherwise the data will be copied.

*Fill Handle*

> ℹ *It is only possible to drag in one direction at one time, i.e. across a row or down a column.*

## ☞ Manoeuvres

1.  On a blank worksheet enter your first name in **B2**.

2.  Select **B2** and move the mouse pointer to the fill handle of **B2**. Click and drag the cell along to **G2**.

3.  Your name will be copied into the cells and a **Smart Tag** will be displayed. Click the tag to see what options are available for this operation but do not select any.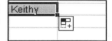

4.  In **C4** enter **January**. Click and drag the fill handle of **C4** along to **G4**.

5.  In **B6** enter today's date in the format **dd/mm/yyyy**.

6.  Click and drag the fill handle of **B6** down to **B12**. The default is to increment each date by one day. Click the **Smart Tag** and select the **Fill Years** option. Each date is now incremented by one year.

7.  Experiment using the fill handle with the following examples:

    | | | |
    |---|---|---|
    | Mon | 9:00 am | Order No 999 |
    | 1-Jan | 1st Quarter | Hello |

8.  Select tab **Sheet2** and enter **123** in cell **C3**. Click and drag the fill handle to cell **F3**. The entry **123** is repeated.

9.  Select cell **C3** hold down the **<Ctrl>** key and click and drag with the fill handle to cell **C11**. The values are incremented.

10. In cell **B14** enter **10** and in cell **C14** enter **15**. Click and drag to highlight the range **B14:C14**. Use the **Fill Handle** for the selected range to click and drag to cell **H14**. The values are incremented by the original step (**5**).

11. Close the workbook <u>without</u> saving.

# Driving Lesson 44 - Copying Cells

## ⊞ Park and Read

Rather than repeatedly typing the same data into several cells, the **Copy** command can be used to copy labels, values and formulas. The selected cells are placed in an area of *Windows* called the **Clipboard**, from there they can be **Pasted** to other locations.

## ☞ Manoeuvres

1.  On an empty worksheet, click on cell **B3**, type **HELLO** then press **<Enter>**.

2.  To copy this cell, click on cell **B3** and then click the **Copy** button, 📋.

ⓘ *The menu command* **Edit | Copy** *or the key press* **<Ctrl C>** *can be used instead of the* **Copy** *button,* 📋.

ⓘ *Excel places a* **Marquee** *(a moving dashed line) around the selected cell(s) to show which cells are to be copied. Notice that the message* **Select destination and press ENTER or choose Paste** *is displayed in the* **Status Bar**.

3.  Move to cell **B7** and press **<Enter>**. The contents of **B3** will now be pasted into **B7**. The contents of **B3** will remain unchanged. Note that **B3** no longer has a dashed line around it.

4.  Enter **65** into cell **C6** and with cell **C6** active, click the **Copy** button.

5.  Move to **B9** and click the **Paste** button, 📋▾. The value is pasted into the new location and a **Smart Tag**, 📋 is displayed. Click the tag to see a list of options concerning the pasting process. Do not select any.

ⓘ *The menu command* **Edit | Paste** *or the key press* **<Ctrl V>** *can be used instead of the* **Paste** *button,* 📋▾.

6.  Note that **C6** still has a dashed line, indicating that its contents can be pasted again if required. Move to **B10** and paste again. Press **<Esc>** to end the pasting and remove the dashed line around **C6**.

ⓘ *The* **Paste** *command is used for pasting repeatedly, the* **<Enter>** *key is used to paste a single copy and to end the copy process.*

# Driving Lesson 44 - Continued

7.   Select **Edit | Office Clipboard** to display the **Clipboard Task Pane** if not already shown. The clipboard is common to all *Office* applications, so it may contain many items already. Click 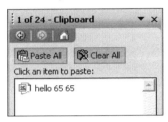 to remove any existing items.

8.   To copy a range, highlight the range **B7:B10** and click the **Copy** button. The values will appear in the **Clipboard Task Pane**.

9.   As well as using the **Paste** button or the <**Enter**> key, items can be pasted directly from the **Clipboard**. Click the destination cell, **H5**, which will become the top left cell of the pasted range and then click the entry in the **Clipboard** to paste the range.

10.  Cells can be copied from sheet to sheet within the same book and can be pasted more than once from the **Clipboard**.

11.  Click the **Sheet3** tab at the bottom of the worksheet area to display that sheet.

12.  Click on cell **A2** and then click the entry in the **Clipboard** to paste the range. The four cells from **Sheet1** are copied to **Sheet3**.

13.  Click back on **Sheet1** to check that the original range is still present.

14.  Close the workbook <u>without</u> saving.

# Driving Lesson 45 - Moving Cells

## ▣ Park and Read

The **Cut** and **Paste** commands allow the user to <u>move</u> the content of a cell or a range of cells to other parts of the worksheet, and to other worksheets.

Care should be taken when moving numbers into cells that are referenced by formulas.

## ↱ Manoeuvres

1.  Start a new workbook.

2.  Enter any two numbers in **E5** and **E6**. In **E7** enter a formula to add the two numbers.

3.  Select the range **E5:E6**. Click the **Cut** button, ✄, to cut the selected cells from the worksheet (they are still there at this point until pasted).

ℹ️ *The menu command **Edit | Cut** or the key press <**Ctrl X**> can be used instead of the **Cut** button.*

4.  Move the pointer to **G7** and click the **Paste** button, 📋. The values appear in the new location and disappear from the original cells, i.e. they are moved.

5.  Notice that the calculation in **E7** is still correct. Click on cell **E7** to see that the calculation now references the new locations.

ℹ️ *Remember that the menu command **Edit | Paste** or the key press <**Ctrl V**> can be used instead of the **Paste** button.*

6.  In **C8** enter the formula **=C6+C7**, the cell should display zero.

7.  Select cell **G7** and **G8**, click with the right mouse button and select **Cut** from the shortcut menu.

8.  Move to cell **C6** right click, and select **Paste.** The result calculated now shows **#REF!** an error message.

ℹ️ *Take care when pasting into cells that contain data as the original information is overwritten. If cells are referenced by formulas those cells are shown as errors.*

9.  Click the **Undo** button to reverse the last paste. Press <**Esc**> to remove the marquee.

# Driving Lesson 45 - Continued

10.  In cell **G9** use **AutoSum** to add the two numbers. These three cells can be cut or copied and pasted on the same sheet.

11.  Highlight the range **G7:G9** and select to **Cut**.

12.  Click on cell **B3** and use **Paste** to place the three cells. Click on cell **B5** and note the formula references the two cells directly above.

$\boxed{\mathbf{i}}$ *Cells or ranges that are **Cut** also appear on the **Clipboard** as with the **Copy** function, but if they are pasted from there, the original entries are NOT removed from the **Clipboard**.*

13.  As well as moving cells on the same sheet they can also be moved between sheets in the same book. Highlight the range **B3:B5** and click **Cut**.

14.  Select the **Sheet2** tab, click on cell **H4** and click **Paste**. The cell contents are removed from **Sheet1** and placed on **Sheet3**. Check both **Sheet1** and **Sheet2**.

15.  Close the **Clipboard** by clicking the **Close** button.

16.  On **Sheet1** delete the cell contents of cell **C8** and **E7**. The sheet should now be blank.

17.  Close the open workbook <u>without</u> saving.

# Driving Lesson 46 - Copying & Moving between Workbooks

## ⓟ Park and Read

The cells can also be copied or moved from workbook to workbook.

## ⋔ Manoeuvres

1.    Open the workbooks **League** (world hockey leagues) and **Survey** (an analysis of 220 hockey fans and whether they replied to a survey).

2.    A sample of 20 people from the survey has been requested. In the **Survey** workbook, highlight the range from **A:G** of 20 rows from anywhere in the survey and select to **Copy** using any method.

3.    Click on the **League** workbook name on the **Taskbar** or select **Window** and click **League** to display the **League** workbook.

4.    Click on the **Sheet2** tab.

5.    Click on cell **C5** (the cell to place the copy) and then press <**Enter**>. The range is copied from **Survey** to **Sheet2** in the **League** workbook.

ℹ️ *The data is not fully displayed because the columns are not wide enough. The widening of columns is covered later. Leave it for now.*

6.    Make **Survey** the active workbook and close it <u>without</u> saving.

ℹ️ *Single cells are copied from sheet to sheet and book to book in exactly the same way as a range.*

ℹ️ *The **Clipboard** can also be used to copy and paste information between any Microsoft Office application.*

7.    Not only can cells be moved between sheets they can be moved between workbooks. Display the workbook **League, Sheet1**. Highlight the range **A32:I50** (the last 2 leagues). Select to **Cut**.

8.    Start a new workbook and on **Sheet1** make the active cell **A2** and **Paste** the cells. This moves the cells to a different workbook.

9.    Check back to the workbook **League**, to see if the data has been removed from **Sheet1**.

10.   Copy the contents of **A1** (the title) and select the new workbook. **Paste** the copied contents in **A1**. Left align the label.

11.   Save the new workbook as **Lower Leagues** and close it.

12.   Close the workbook **League** <u>without</u> saving.

# Driving Lesson 47 - Finding Specific Text

## ▣ Park and Read

Specific text can be found in formulas, labels, comments, etc. and even replaced if necessary. The search starts at the active cell.

## ↱ Manoeuvres

1.  Open the workbook **Hotel**.

2.  With **A1** the active cell, select **Edit | Find**.

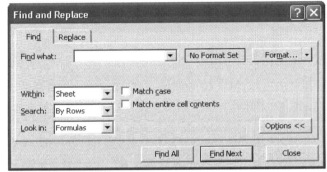

ℹ️ *If a simpler version of this box appears, click the **Options** button to display this version. Available choices are whether to search by row or column, whether the text is part or all of the cell content, and whether the text case is important.*

3.  In the **Find what** box, enter **Daily Rate** and click on **Find Next**.

4.  The active cell will now be **R3**, the **Daily Rate**.

ℹ️ *It may be necessary to move the **Find** dialog box so that the results of the search can be seen.*

5.  Close the **Find and Replace** dialog box and use the key press <**Ctrl Home**> to move to cell **A1**.

6.  Find **Tax**. Select **By Rows** in the **Search** box, if not already selected. Click on **Find Next**.

7.  The active cell will be **Q22**, the **Tax Rates** label. To find any other occurrences of **Tax**, click on **Find Next**.

8.  The active cell is now **A36**, the **Company Tax**.

9.  Click **Find Next**. There should be no others. **Close** the dialog box.

10. Leave the workbook open as it is used in the next Driving Lesson.

# Driving Lesson 48 - Replacing Text

## Park and Read

In a similar manner to finding text, it can be found then replaced.

## Manoeuvres

1.   Use **Hotel**, with **A1** the active cell, select **Edit | Replace**. Ensure that the full version of the dialog box is displayed. Click **Options** if necessary.

2.   In the **Find what** box, enter **room** and in **Replace with**, enter **chamber**.

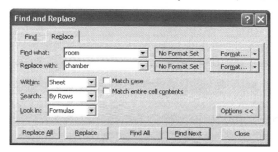

3.   Ensure that **Match case** is not checked and select **Replace All**.

*It may be necessary to move the **Replace** dialog box so that the affected cells can be seen.*

4.   All occurrences of **Room** have now been replaced with **Chamber**. Click **OK** at the confirmation message.

5.   In the **Find what** box, enter **chamber**, and in **Replace with** enter **room**.

6.   Click on **Find Next**. The first occurrence of **chamber** is highlighted. Click on **Replace** to change it to **room**.

7.   Continue clicking **Replace** to change all of the chambers back to rooms.

8.   When all are replaced a message dialog box is displayed.

9.   Click **OK** and then close the **Replace** dialog box.

10.  Close the workbook <u>without</u> saving.

# Driving Lesson 49 - Sorting

## ▣ Park and Read

In a list, the rows can be arranged in a specific order using the column headings, C, D, etc., or column titles, e.g. a header row or labels, as a reference. The **Sort Ascending** button, [A↓] and the **Sort Descending** button, [Z↓], on the **Standard Toolbar** can be used to sort information. The rows are sorted automatically on the column containing the active cell.

## ⌒ Manoeuvres

1.    Start a new workbook.

2.    Enter a column of 8 names (surnames or first names) starting in cell **B3**.

3.    Sort the names into ascending alphabetic order, click in an occupied cell in column **B** and then click the **Sort Ascending** button, [A↓].

4.    With the active cell still in column **B** click the **Sort Descending** button, [Z↓]. The names are sorted into descending order.

5.    Add ages (in years) in column **C** adjacent to the names.

6.    To sort the ages list into ascending order, click in an occupied cell in column **C** and click the **Sort Ascending** button, [A↓]. The ages are sorted in ascending order with the names in column **B** kept with correct ages.

7.    Sort the ages into descending order.

ℹ️ *More complicated sorting can be carried out using the **Data | Sort** command, via the **Sort** dialog box.*

8.    Close the workbook <u>without</u> saving.

# Driving Lesson 50 - Revision

This Driving Lesson covers the features introduced in this section. Try not to refer to the preceding Driving Lessons while completing it.

1. Open the workbook **Home Finances**.

2. Examine your finances to decide whether you can afford to buy a new camera, costing £90, for your holiday in August. Go to cell **N16** and look at your total savings for the end of the year. They are estimated to be less than you need to buy that camera, so drastic action is needed if you do not want to owe money at the end of the year.

3. From the beginning of January you decide to stop using your car and save petrol by cycling to work for three months. Select the range of cells for **Petrol** expenses from **Jan** through to **Mar**. As you feel extremely health conscious you decide to extend your cycling through to July, use the <Shift> key to extend the range to **Jul** and clear the cell contents.

4. Check **N16**. How much savings do you now have?

5. This good news is short lived as you realise that you do not own a bike and will have to continue to use the car. Click the **Undo** button to put the figures for your petrol back into the worksheet.

6. You now decide to limit your **Leisure** expenses to a maximum of £50 per month from **Jan** through to **Jul**. Type **50** in **Jan Leisure** (cell **B7**) and use the fill handle to copy this through to **Jul**.

| | A | B | C | D | E | F | G | H | I |
|---|---|---|---|---|---|---|---|---|---|
| 1 | House Finance | Jan | Feb | Mar | Apr | May | Jun | Jul | Aug |
| 2 | Pay | 415 | 415 | 415 | 415 | 415 | 415 | 415 | 415 |
| 3 | Other Income | 0 | 0 | 0 | 0 | 0 | 0 | 0 | 0 |
| 4 | Total Income | 415 | 415 | 415 | 415 | 415 | 415 | 415 | 415 |
| 5 | Rent | 80 | 80 | 80 | 80 | 80 | 80 | 80 | 90 |
| 6 | Holidays | 0 | 0 | 0 | 50 | 0 | 0 | 0 | 210 |
| 7 | Leisure | 50 | 50 | 50 | 50 | 50 | 50 | 50 | 187 |
| 8 | Electricity | 49 | 0 | 0 | 43 | 0 | 0 | 29 | 0 |
| 9 | Gas | 46 | 0 | 0 | 51 | 0 | 0 | 32 | 0 |
| 10 | Telephone | 0 | 37 | 0 | 0 | 35 | 0 | 0 | 36 |

7. Check **N16**, how much have you now saved?

8. You intend to purchase the camera in July so add **90** to the figure already in **Others** for July.

9. How much will you have in your savings by the end of the year now?

10. Close the workbook <u>without</u> saving.

**i**    *Answers to this revision exercise can be found at the end of this guide.*

If you experienced any difficulty completing this Revision refer back to the Driving Lessons in this section. Then redo the Revision.

# Driving Lesson 51 - Revision

This Driving Lesson covers the features introduced in this section. Try not to refer to the preceding Driving Lessons while completing it.

1.  Create a blank spreadsheet. Enter **February** in **B2**, **Week 1** in **C3** and **Mon** in **B4**. Use the **Fill Handle** to produce the following sheet.

| | A | B | C | D | E | F | G |
|---|---|---|---|---|---|---|---|
| 1 | | | | | | | |
| 2 | | February | | | | | |
| 3 | | | Week 1 | Week 2 | Week 3 | Week 4 | Week 5 |
| 4 | | Mon | | | | | |
| 5 | | Tue | | | | | |
| 6 | | Wed | | | | | |
| 7 | | Thu | | | | | |
| 8 | | Fri | | | | | |
| 9 | | Sat | | | | | |
| 10 | | Sun | | | | | |
| 11 | | | | | | | |

2.  The first day of **February 2003** was a **Saturday**. Type **01/02/03** into cell **C9**. Use the **Fill Handle** to drag **C9** to **C10**.

3.  Enter **03/02/03** in cell **D4**, **10/02/03** in cell **E4**, **17/02/03** in cell **F4 and 24/02/03** in cell **G4**.

4.  Fill the blank days of the week using the **Fill Handle**. What day of the week was the last day of **February** and was **2003** a leap year?

5.  In cell **B13** type **Year**. In cell **B14** type the year you were born, e.g. **1983**.

6.  Use the **<Ctrl>** key to fill the cells below **B14** by dragging down the column until the series of dates reaches the present year.

7.  In cell **C13** type **Age** and in cell **C14** type **0**, as you were born in that year.

8.  Fill the column down increasing the series by **1** each time until you reach the current year. You should now see how old you will be this year.

9.  In cell **D13** type **Days Old**. In cell **D14** type **0** and in **D15** type **365**. Highlight the two numbers and use the **Fill Handle** to fill down the column. Remember that this is an approximate figure as no account is taken for leap years.

10. Continue to increase the series in column **C** until **65**. Increase column **B** and **D** also to match column **C**. How many days old will you be or were you when **65** years old?

11. Close the workbook <u>without</u> saving.

If you experienced any difficulty completing this Revision refer back to the Driving Lessons in this section. Then redo the Revision.

Once you are confident with the features, complete the Record of Achievement Matrix referring to the section at the end of the guide. Only when competent move on to the next Section.

# Section 7
# Printing

## By the end of this Section you should be able to:

**Print a Worksheet and Workbook**

**Use Print Preview**

**Change the Page Setup**

**Add Headers and Footers**

**Use Print Titles**

**Display and Print Formulas**

**Print Specified Areas of a Worksheet**

To gain an understanding of the above features, work through the **Driving Lessons** in this **Section**.

For each **Driving Lesson**, read the **Park and Read** instructions, without touching the keyboard, then work through the numbered steps of the **Manoeuvres** on the computer. Complete the **Revision Exercise(s)** at the end of the section to test your knowledge.

# Driving Lesson 52 - Printing

## 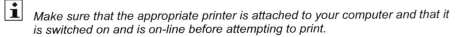 Park and Read

Worksheets can be printed out to give a hard copy. It is possible to decide what to print: the sheet, the pages printed and the number of copies.

It is customary to **Print Preview** the worksheet before printing, as it may not fit on the paper, as you need it to.

## Manoeuvres

1.　Open the workbook **Company**. This is a small worksheet and therefore fits easily on one piece of paper.

**i**　*Make sure that the appropriate printer is attached to your computer and that it is switched on and is on-line before attempting to print.*

2.　Select **File | Print** or use the key press **<Ctrl P>** to display the **Print** dialog box. The bottom part of the dialog box controls what is printed.

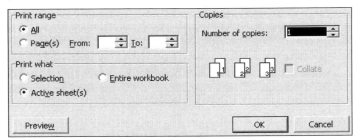

3.　The default settings are **All** for the **Print range**, **Active sheet(s)** for **Print what** and **1** for the **Number of copies**. Click **OK** to print one copy of the worksheet.

4.　When the worksheet will print as required, the **Print** dialog box can be bypassed by clicking on the **Print** button. This uses the default settings described above and prints a single copy. Click the **Print** button, 🖨.

5.　All the worksheets in a workbook can be printed. Select **File | Print** and under **Print what** select the **Entire workbook** option and click **OK**. The two sheets are printed.

6.　Close the workbook <u>without</u> saving.

**i**　*It is usual to **Print Preview** the worksheet before printing, as it may not fit on the paper and **Page Setup** many need to be used to fit the worksheet to the paper size. These topics are covered in the following Driving Lessons.*

# Driving Lesson 53 - Print Preview

## ▣ Park and Read

**Print Preview** is used before printing to show the layout of the worksheet on the page(s). Changing **Page Setup** and **Printing** can both be done within **Print Preview**.

## ⬧ Manoeuvres

1.    Open the workbook **Exam Results** and select **File | Print Preview** or click the **Print Preview** button, ▣.

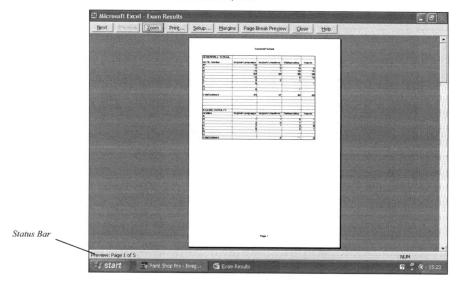

*Status Bar*

2.    This shows how the worksheet will be printed. The worksheet covers five pages. Look on the **Status Bar**, it displays **Preview: Page 1 of 5**. Click the **Next** button to view the second page.

3.    The **Next** and **Previous** buttons are used to view the rest of the pages of a multi-page worksheet. This is a five page document. Return to **Page 1**.

4.    The key presses <**Page Up**> and <**Page Down**> can also be used to view other pages. Use <**Page Down**> to move to **Page 3**. Use <**Page Up**> to return to **Page 1**.

ℹ *The **Print** button within **Print Preview** is used when the preview is satisfactory.*

5.    Click the **Close** button to close **Print Preview** but leave the workbook open for the next Driving Lesson.

# Driving Lesson 54 - Page Setup

## ▣ Park and Read

**Page Setup** is used to change the way a worksheet is displayed on the pages. Pages can be printed in either **Portrait** or **Landscape** view or can be scaled to fit on a number of pages.

## Manoeuvres

1.  Use the workbook **Exam Results**.

2.  To change the appearance of the worksheet before it is printed select **File | Page Setup**.

3.  The **Page Setup** dialog box has four option tabs. Click the **Page** tab, if this is not selected already.

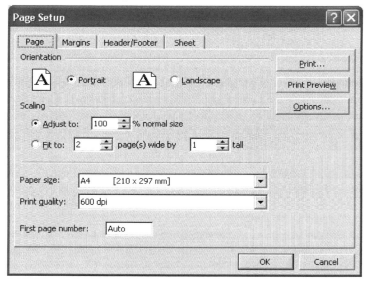

4.  There are three main areas, **Orientation**, **Scaling** and **Paper size**. Make sure that the **Portrait** option is selected and click .

5.  Notice there are **5** pages. Click the **Setup** button to return to **Page Setup**.

6.  Select the **Landscape** option.

7.  Click **OK** to close **Page Setup** and return to **Print Preview**.

# Driving Lesson 56 - Continued

8.   There are three pages, notice that **Landscape** is where the largest edge of the paper is at the top. Use the **Next** and **Previous** buttons to view all the pages.

9.   Click the **Setup** button to return to **Page Setup**.

10.  Use the **Fit to** option in **Scaling** to fit the worksheet to a set number of pages, e.g. **1 page(s) wide by 1 tall** will print the worksheet on a single page. Select to fit the worksheet onto a single page.

> **i**  *The **Fit to** option can be set to any number of required pages, e.g. **1** wide by **3** tall. The worksheet will be scaled to fit within the 3 pages. It may occupy less pages but not more.*

11.  Click **OK** to close **Page Setup** and return to **Print Preview**. The worksheet is placed on one page. It is a little difficult to read.

12.  Click the **Setup** button to return to **Page Setup** and select the **Adjust to** option and change back to **100%** by either typing in the value or using ⬆⬇.

13.  The default **Paper size** is **A4**, but this can be changed if working with different sized paper. Click the drop down arrow to the right of **A4**.

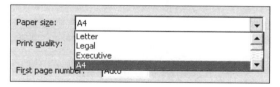

> **i**  *The actual **Paper size** options available will depend on the model of printer in use.*

14.  Examine the list and then select **A5**. Click **OK** to close **Page Setup** and return to **Print Preview**. The worksheet is now on 10 pages.

15.  Click the **Setup** button to return to **Page Setup** and change the paper size back to **A4**. Click **OK** to close **Page Setup** and return to **Print Preview**.

16.  Close **Print Preview** but leave the workbook open.

# Driving Lesson 55 - Margins

## ▣ Park and Read

**Margins** can be reduced or enlarged to give more or less white space around a worksheet. Margins are normally reduced to allow more of a worksheet to fit on each piece of paper.

## ↱ Manoeuvres

1.   Use the workbook **Exam Results**.

2.   Select **File | Page Setup** and then select the **Margins** tab.

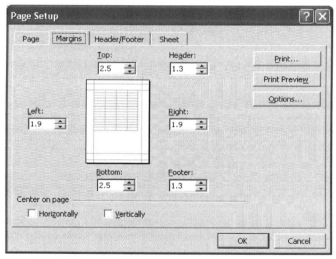

3.   To change **Margin** settings (values are in centimetres), either type in the values or use ⬍ to increase or decrease the values within the **Top**, **Bottom**, **Left** and **Right** boxes. The worksheet is **Landscape** and fits across three pages; reduce the **Left** margin down to **0.4** by clicking in the box and changing the amount.

4.   Change the **Right** margin down to **0.4** by clicking three times on the down spinner (the down triangle).

5.   Click the **Print Preview** button to view the changes. There are now only two pages. Click the **Setup** button.

6.   Clicking in the **Center on page** boxes centres the worksheet horizontally and/or vertically. Select the option **Vertically**. Click **OK** to return to **Print Preview** to view the change.

7.   Close **Print Preview** and close **Exam Results** <u>without</u> saving.

# Driving Lesson 56 - Printing a Selection

## ▣ Park and Read

It is possible to print just a part of a worksheet, a selected range for example. You might want to do this when only a small area of the worksheet is relevant for your intended audience.

## ⌒ Manoeuvres

1.   Open the workbook **Hotel**.

2.   Select the range **A3:E17,** i.e. the first four months of receipts.

3.   Select **File | Print** or use the key press <**Ctrl P**> to display the **Print** dialog box.

4.   Ensure **Print what** is set to **Selection**.

5.   Click **OK** to print the selected range.

ℹ️ *The selection can be previewed but only after the **Selection** option has been chosen.*

6.   Close the workbook <u>without</u> saving.

# Driving Lesson 57 - Headers and Footers

## 🅿 Park and Read

**Headers** and **Footers** are lines of text which appear at the top/bottom of every printed page. They can contain text or field codes in the three areas: **Left section**, **Center section** and **Right section**.

## 🠔 Manoeuvres

1. Open the workbook **League**. This is a workbook that contains various hockey leagues, similar to the World Cup in football.

2. Select **File | Page Setup** and click the **Header/Footer** tab and click the **Custom Header** button.

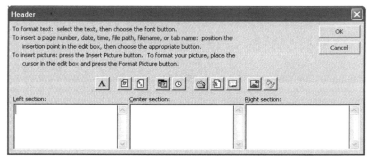

3. Place the cursor in the **Center section** and type **World Hockey Tables**.

4. Place the cursor in the **Right section** and type **Provisional**.

5. Click **OK** then **OK** again to complete the **Header**.

6. **Print Preview** the worksheet with the new header. View the two pages to see the header on both pages. The title on row 1 of the worksheet is now duplicated by the **Header** on page one.

ℹ️ *When adding a title choose between using a cell on the worksheet or a **Header**.*

7. Close **Print Preview** and select **File | Page Setup** and click on the **Header/Footer** tab.

8. Click the **Custom Header** button. Edit the centre text to **World Hockey League Tables**. Delete the text in the right section to remove it. Click **OK**.

9. Click the **Custom Footer** button.

ℹ️ *There are various buttons that place field codes into **Footers** (these also apply when creating **Headers**).*

# Driving Lesson 57 - Continued

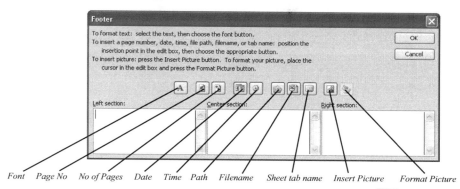

Font    Page No    No of Pages    Date    Time    Path    Filename    Sheet tab name    Insert Picture    Format Picture

10. Click in the **Left section** and then click the **Date** button, ![date], this places the field code **&[Date]** in the box. This code displays the current date whenever the worksheet is printed. Add a space and then click the **Time** button, ![time] to add the current time.

11. Click in the **Center section** and type **Page** (followed by a space) and click the **Page number** button, ![page]. *Excel* places the field code **&[Page]** in the box.

12. Click in the **Right section** and click the **Sheet tab** button, ![tab], press / and then click the **File Name** button, ![file]. The field codes are **&[Tab]** and **&[File]**. This identifies the printout, it displays the sheet and book names.

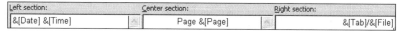

*To delete a field in a **Header/Footer**, select the field code and press <**Delete**>.*

13. Click on **OK** to close the **Footer** dialog box, then click the **Custom Header** button.

14. Highlight the text **World Hockey League Tables** in the **Center section** (added in step 3). The text can be modified, click the **Font** button, ![A]. In the **Font** dialog box, click **Bold** under **Font Style** and either type or select **16** in the **Size** box. The title is bigger and bold. Click **OK** three times.

15. **Print Preview** the worksheet to see the new **Header** and **Footer**. Click the footer area to zoom in to that part of the page. Click again to zoom out. Check each part of the **Footer**. Check both pages.

16. Click the **Setup** button. The worksheet has two **Landscape** pages. Click the **Page** tab and change to **Portrait**. Click **OK** to return to **Print Preview**. The worksheet should only be one page. Close **Print Preview**.

17. Save the workbook as **League2** and close it.

# Driving Lesson 58 - Print Titles

## 🅿 Park and Read

Rows and columns of the worksheet may be specified as titles, and these can be displayed on each printed page. This is often used to show labels on each page.

## ☞ Manoeuvres

1.  Open the workbook **Survey**.

2.  Select **File | Page Setup** and click the **Sheet** tab.

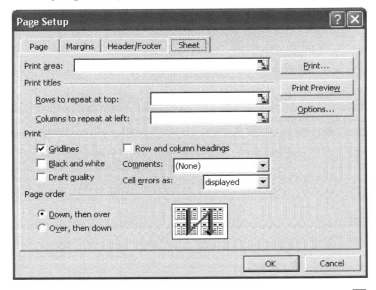

3.  Click in the **Rows to repeat at top** box, click the **Collapse** button, 📇 and select rows **1** to **5** (the dialog box may have to be moved to do this). Click to expand the dialog box and then select **OK**.

4.  **Print Preview** the worksheet. Use the **Next** and **Previous** buttons to see the other pages. Notice that the first five rows of the worksheet are repeated on every page.

ℹ️ *Columns to repeat at left can be set for worksheets that are short and wide. Both rows and columns cannot be set as Print titles at the same time.*

5.  Close **Print Preview** and close the workbook <u>without</u> saving.

ℹ️ *Print titles cannot be set using Setup from within Print Preview.*

# Driving Lesson 59 - Print Options

## ▣ Park and Read

The **Print** dialog box includes options that control what and how information is printed. **Print Preview** is used to check that the layout is correct prior to printing.

## ☞ Manoeuvres

1.  Open the workbook **League2**.

2.  Select **File | Print** or use the key press **<Ctrl P>** to display the **Print** dialog box.

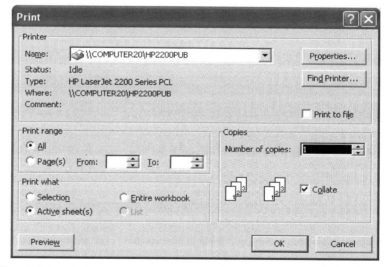

3.  The **Print what** options allows you either to print a **Selection** (a highlighted range on worksheet), **Active sheet(s)** (the current worksheet) or **Entire workbook** (all the sheets in the workbook). Make sure **Active sheet(s)** is selected.

4.  The **Number of copies** is set at **1**. This option is changed when more copies are required. Change **Number of copies** to **2**.

ⓘ *This worksheet fits on one page. Selected pages of larger worksheets are printed using the **From, To Page(s)** option under **Print range**. For a single page use the same number, e.g. **From 1 To 1**.*

5.  To print two copies of the active worksheet click **OK**.

6.  Close the workbook **League2** <u>without</u> saving.

# Driving Lesson 60 - Displaying & Printing Formulas

## ▣ Park and Read

Instead of formula results, the actual formulas themselves can be displayed on screen and then printed. This is useful when checking that formulas are correct.

## ☞ Manoeuvres

1.  Open the workbook **Formulas**, which contains some simple calculations.

2.  Enter **6** in cell **B4**. Is the answer correct in **B6**? Click on cell **B6**. Check the **Formula Bar** for the formula.

3.  To display all the formulas on a worksheet to check them, select **Tools | Options**, make sure that the **View** tab is selected and check the **Formulas** box under **Window options**.

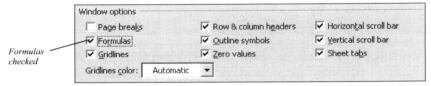

*Formulas checked*

4.  Click **OK** to close **Options** and return to the worksheet. The formulas are displayed (the columns are widened to display more text). If the **Formula Auditing** toolbar appears, close it.

5.  There is a problem with cell **D6**, it contains the number **10**. Enter the formula to multiply the two numbers **=D4*D5**.

6.  To turn the **Formula** display on and off using the menus is time consuming. A key press, **<Ctrl `>**, can be used. This is **Ctrl** and the key to the left of the **1** key and under the **Escape <Esc>** key. Press **<Ctrl `>**. The formulas are no longer displayed.

7.  Press **<Ctrl `>** to display the formulas.

8.  If this worksheet was printed, it would be difficult to check if the rows and columns were correct. To help with checking, the headings and the gridlines can also be printed. Select **File | Page Setup** and choose the **Sheet** tab. Check **Row and column headings** and **Gridlines**.

9.  Click the **Print Preview** button to see the formulas and the headings with the gridlines displayed.

10.  Click the **Print** button, then click **OK** to print a copy of the worksheet.

11.  Close the workbook <u>without</u> saving.

# Driving Lesson 61 - Revision

This Driving Lesson covers the features introduced in this section. Try not to refer to the preceding Driving Lessons while completing it.

1.  Open the workbook **Oscar**.

2.  **Print Preview** the worksheet.

3.  Add the header **Oscar Winners** and insert page numbering in the footer.

4.  Change the page orientation to **Landscape**.

5.  Change the top and bottom, margins to **2.0**.

6.  Change the left and right margins to **0.4**.

7.  Select and print the last 10 Oscar winning films only.

8.  Change the **Page Setup** options to print the titles.

9.  Print a copy of the worksheet.

10. Close the workbook <u>without</u> saving.

If you experienced any difficulty completing this Revision refer back to the Driving Lessons in this section. Then redo the Revision.

# Driving Lesson 62 - Revision

This Driving Lesson covers the features introduced in this section. Try not to refer to the preceding Driving Lessons while completing it.

1.    Open the workbook **Hotel**.

2.    Alter the page setup for printing to the following:

        Header -        Change to **Company Finances** (centred)

        Footer -        Remove the word **Page** to leave just the page number

        Margins -      **Top** and **Bottom 2cm** and **Left** and **Right 1cm**

3.    **Print Preview** the worksheet.

4.    Print out **Page 2** only.

5.    Using **Page Setup**, select to repeat **Column A**.

6.    Select the range **F3:J14** and print the selection.

7.    Close the workbook <u>without</u> saving.

8.    Open the workbook **Company**. This is a small workbook containing two worksheets, **Actual** and **Forecast**.

9.    The worksheets are very similar and it is difficult to identify which is which from the printed copies. Add a centred sheet tab code to each of the worksheets in the footer.

10.   Print a copy of the entire workbook.

11.   Close the **Company** workbook <u>without</u> saving.

If you experienced any difficulty completing this Revision refer back to the Driving Lessons in this section. Then redo the Revision.

Once you are confident with the features, complete the Record of Achievement Matrix referring to the section at the end of the guide. Only when competent move on to the next Section.

# Section 8
# Formatting

## By the end of this Section you should be able to:

**Format Numbers, Dates & Percentages**

**Change Cell Alignment and Rotate Text**

**Add Borders and Colour**

**Change Row Height and Column Width**

**Insert and Delete Rows and Columns**

**Use Freeze & Zoom**

**Use the Format Painter**

To gain an understanding of the above features, work through the **Driving Lessons** in this **Section**.

For each **Driving Lesson**, read the **Park and Read** instructions, without touching the keyboard, then work through the numbered steps of the **Manoeuvres** on the computer. Complete the **Revision Exercise(s)** at the end of the section to test your knowledge.

# Driving Lesson 63 - Formatting

## ▣ Park and Read

To **Format** is to change the way cells look in order to improve the overall appearance of a worksheet. The **Format Menu** is used to achieve the full range of formatting. However, the **Formatting Toolbar** provides buttons to format more quickly.

Formatting can change the style, size, colour, alignment and number format of text and numbers, the border style, colour and pattern of cells.

## ⟲ Manoeuvres

1.   Open the workbook **Climate**.

2.   Select **Format | Cells**. The cells to be formatted (cell or range) would normally be selected before using this command, but is used here for observation only.

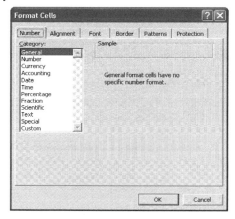

3.   The **Format Cells** dialog box is displayed. This is a six tabbed dialog box.

4.   The **Number** tab is the first, if this is not displayed, click **Number**. This tab controls the way numbers are shown, including dates and times.

5.   Click **Alignment**, this positions information in cells. Click **Font**, this changes the text style, size and other text features.

6.   Click **Border**, this controls lines around cells. Click **Patterns**, this controls background cell colour. Click **Protection**, this is part of a system to stop information being lost.

7.   Click **Cancel** to close the **Format Cells** dialog box.

8.   Leave the workbook open for the next Driving Lesson.

# Driving Lesson 64 - Bold, Underline & Italic

## 🅿 Park and Read

The easiest way to make a cell stand out is to make it **Bold**. This works well with titles.

<u>Underline</u> is a line under the cell contents (not a cell border).

*Italic* gives you leaning text, similar to handwriting.

## 🏲 Manoeuvres

1.    Use the workbook **Climate**.

2.    Select the cells **B2:K2**.

3.    To make this range of cells **Bold**, click the **Bold** button, **B**, on the **Formatting Toolbar**.

> ℹ️ *The button is displayed with a blue border when the feature is active. This applies to all formatting buttons.*

4.    Select the cells **A2:A18** and click once on the following buttons, **Italic**, *I* and **Underline**, **U**.

5.    Click anywhere on the worksheet to remove the highlighted selection and see the results. The underlining of a column of labels is not very effective.

6.    Select cells **A2:A18** again and click the **Underline** button, **U**, again to turn off the underlining. Click anywhere on the worksheet to remove the highlighted section.

7.    There are quick key presses for bold, italic and underline. Click on cell **A2**. Press <**Ctrl B**> to add **Bold**, and to add **Underline**, press <**Ctrl U**>. The key press for **Italic** is <**Ctrl I**>, this cell already has **Italic** added.

8.    The same keys turn off the formatting. Press <**Ctrl I**> and <**Ctrl U**> to turn off italic and underline for cell **A2**.

> ℹ️ *The **Font** tab within the **Format | Cells** command could have been used to apply this formatting but the buttons and key presses are quicker.*

9.    To double underline the contents of cell **A2**, select **Format | Cells** and click the **Font** tab. Click the drop down arrow of the **Underline** box and select **Double**. Click **OK** to apply the formatting.

10.   Leave the workbook open for the next Driving Lesson.

# Driving Lesson 65 - Fonts & Font Size

## Park and Read

A **Font** is a type or style of print. Examples of fonts are Arial, Times New Roman, Modern, *Script*, etc. The default font and font size is **Arial 10**. **Font Size** is measured in points, more points means a larger size.

## Manoeuvres

1.  Using the workbook **Climate**, highlight the cells **B2:K2**, select **Format | Cells** and the **Font** tab.

2.  Choose any **Font** from the **Font** box and view the results in the **Preview** box. Repeat to view other **Fonts**.

3.  Select **Times New Roman** and click **OK** to add the formatting.

4.  Select cell **A2**, the title. To change the font, a selection can be made using the drop down list (the down triangle) on the **Formatting** toolbar, 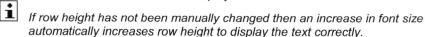. This is quicker when applying a different font. Change the font to **Algerian** (if not available, any other font).

5.  To make the titles bigger you can change the **Font Size**. With cell **A2** still selected, change the size by clicking on the drop down **Font Size** box, [10 ▼], on the **Formatting Toolbar**.

6.  Select **14**. Clicking on the **10** and typing **14** also works. This is especially useful when a size is not displayed in the list.

> **ℹ** *If row height has not been manually changed then an increase in font size automatically increases row height to display the text correctly.*

7.  Select cells **B2:K2**. To change the font size select **Format | Cells**, the **Font** tab and from the **Size** box try a variety of different font sizes and view the results in the **Preview** box. Change the **Size** to **11** and click **OK**.

8.  The formatting on any cell can be copied to other cell(s) using the **Format Painter**. Click on cell **B2**, click the **Format Painter** button, [⬚] and then click and drag the range **B3:K4**. On release of the mouse button the formats from cell **B2** are painted to the range **B3:K4**.

9.  Check that the cells in the range **B3:K4** are **Times New Roman** font, size **11**pt and **bold** (the labels are not fully displayed).

> **ℹ** *To use the **Format Painter** repeatedly, double click when selecting it and when finished painting the format, press <**Esc**> to turn it off.*

10. Leave the workbook open for the next Driving Lesson.

# Driving Lesson 66 - Format Number

##  Park and Read

**Numbers** can be displayed in various styles, with decimal places, including a £ sign, % signs, with or without a separator to indicate thousands, etc.

## Manoeuvres

1.  Use the workbook **Climate** and select the range **B5:K16**.

2.  Select **Format | Cells**. With the **Number** tab selected, click on each of the categories, to see the type of formatting available in each.

3.  Select **Number** from the **Category** list.

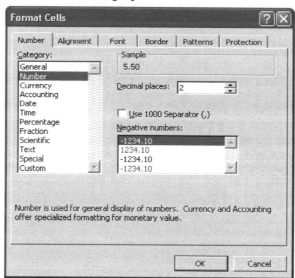

4.  Check that the number of **Decimal places** is set as **2**. Leaving the **Use 1000 Separator (,)** unchecked, displays numbers <u>without</u> the comma separator for thousands.

*In the section **Negative numbers** there are options to display any negative values in red, with or without a minus sign. Above this section is a check box **Use 1000 Separator (,)** which is used to add commas to numbers displaying thousands, e.g. **5,600**.*

5.  Click **OK** to apply the chosen formats. All the numbers in the range are now formatted to two decimal places <u>without</u> the thousands separator.

# Driving Lesson 66 - Continued

6. There are also buttons on the toolbar to **Increase Decimal** places,  and **Decrease Decimal** places, 📊, by one place for each click. With the cells **B5:K16** still selected, click the **Decrease Decimal** button, 📊. The numbers are displayed with one decimal place.

 *After applying number formats, cells may display* **#######**. *This means that the number is too big for the cell. The data is not lost but the column must be widened. This is covered in Driving Lesson 69.*

7. Close the workbook <u>without</u> saving.

8. Open the workbook **Budget**. This workbook contains cells with large numbers and currency values.

9. Highlight the range **B7:N7**. To format this range as numbers with comma separators, select **Format | Cells** and from the **Number** tab, click **Number** in the **Category** list. Change the **Decimal places** to **0** and check **Use 1000 Separator (,)**. Click **OK**.

10. The tax rates are shown as decimals and would be better shown as percentages. Highlight the range **B12:M12**, select **Format | Cells** and from the **Number** tab, click **Percentage** in the **Category** list. Change the **Decimal places** to **0** and click **OK**.

11. The total rows are to be formatted as currency. Highlight the range **B4:N4**, and while holding down the **<Ctrl>** key, select the ranges **B10:N10** and **B14:N14**. The three separate ranges are now highlighted. Select **Format | Cells** and click **Currency** in the **Category** list. Change the **Decimal places** to **0**, add the **£** sign from the **Symbol** drop down list and under **Negative numbers** select to display negative numbers in red with a negative sign.

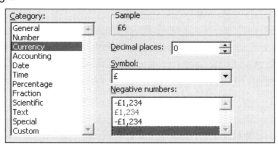

12. Click **OK**.

13. Format the ranges **B2:N2**, **B11:N11** and **B13:N13** as numbers, with no decimal places but with comma separators for thousands.

14. Print a **Landscape** copy of the worksheet, on a single sheet of **A4** paper.

15. Save the workbook as **Budget2** and close it.

# Driving Lesson 67 - Dates

##  Park and Read

**Date** and **Time** are stored as numbers. The **Date** is a number representing the number of days since 1 January 1900. The **Time** is a decimal, as part of a day.

Both the **Date** and **Time** can be displayed in various formats including numbers and text.

## Manoeuvres

1.   Start a new workbook.

2.   In cell **B2** enter your birthday, in the form of **24/2/88**. Press **<Enter>**.

3.   Make **B2** the active cell.

4.   Select **Format | Cells**, choose the **Number** tab.

5.   Select **Date** from the **Category** section and select each format from within **Type**. A preview is available in the **Sample** box.

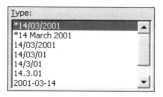

6.   Scroll down the list and select **14 March 2001** format. Click **OK**.

7.   Click in cell **B4** and enter today's date by pressing **<Ctrl ;>**. This is the quick key press for the current date, it is entered as text. Press **<Enter>** to complete the entry.

8.   Repeat the above steps to display today's date in a different format.

9.   Click in cell **B6** and enter the current time by pressing **<Ctrl Shift ;>** Press **<Enter>**.

10.  Click in cell **B6**.

11.  To change the format of the time select **Format | Cells**, the **Number** tab is selected. The **Category** has **Custom** selected with the **Type** as **hh:mm**.

12.  From **Category** box select **Time,** then select any format and click **OK**.

13.  Close the workbook <u>without</u> saving.

# Driving Lesson 68 - Alignment

## ⊞ Park and Read

**Alignment** is the positioning of text in a cell relative to its edges. By default **Labels** (text) are aligned to the left and **Numbers** to the right.

## ⟰ Manoeuvres

1.  Open the workbook **House**.

2.  Select the range **B3:N3**. To align these titles differently there are 3 buttons on the toolbar: **Align Left**, ▤, **Center**, ▤ and **Align Right**, ▤.

3.  Click the **Center** button, ▤, the labels are centred. Click the **Align Right** button, ▤, the labels are moved to the right.

4.  For more alignment options the **Format | Cells** command is used. Click on cell **A1** and select **Format | Cells** and the **Alignment** tab.

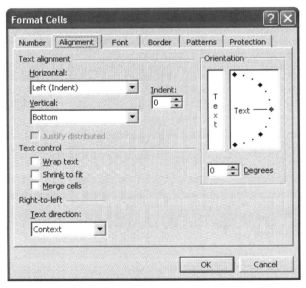

5.  The buttons used above in step 2 are the **Horizontal** options. The options in **Vertical** allow positions **Top**, **Center**, **Bottom**, **Justify** and **Distributed**. From the drop down list in the **Vertical** box, select **Center**.

6.  Click **OK** to apply the formatting. The text is in the centre of the cell, vertically.

# Driving Lesson 68 - Continued

7.   The title is in cell **A1**. To centre it across the width of the worksheet, highlight the range **A1:N1** and click the **Merge and Center** button, ▦, on the **Formatting** toolbar. The cells are merged, with the title in the centre.

**i**  *Alternatively, highlight the range and select Format | Cells, Alignment tab and check Merge cells under Text control. The Merge and Center button can be clicked again to remove the merging and centring that has been applied.*

8.   Rename the sheet as **House Finance**.

9.   Insert a new worksheet.

10.  On the new **Sheet1**, create the following (note that the text **Telephone Extension** is all entered in cell **B3**, it flows into **C3**):

|   | A | B | C | D |
|---|---|---|---|---|
| 1 |   |   |   |   |
| 2 |   |   |   |   |
| 3 | Names | Telephone | Extension |   |
| 4 | John | 356 |   |   |
| 5 | Asif | 871 |   |   |
| 6 | Suzanne | 78 |   |   |
| 7 | Mary | 247 |   |   |
| 8 | Hardeep | 163 |   |   |
| 9 |   |   |   |   |

11.  When the label across the top of a column is too long for the information below, the text can be wrapped within the cell. Click on cell **B3** and select **Format | Cells**, **Alignment** tab and check **Wrap text**.

**i**  *Text wrap can be applied to a range of cells - just select the range first.*

12.  Click **OK**. The text in **B3** is wrapped within the cell and row height is increased automatically. Column **C** can now be used normally.

|   | A | B | C |
|---|---|---|---|
| 1 |   |   |   |
| 2 |   |   |   |
| 3 | Names | Telephone Extension |   |
| 4 | John | 356 |   |
| 5 | Asif | 871 |   |
| 6 | Suzanne | 78 |   |
| 7 | Mary | 247 |   |
| 8 | Hardeep | 163 |   |
| 9 |   |   |   |

**i**  *The row height is only adjusted automatically if it has not been adjusted manually. Row height and column width are covered in the next lessons.*

13.  Save the workbook as **House2** and then close it.

# Driving Lesson 69 - Changing Column Width

## ▣ Park and Read

**Column Width** is the distance across a column. It is measured in units. The size is **8.43** units - do not worry, as column widths are changed by dragging - if it looks right, then it is right.

## ☞ Manoeuvres

1.  Open the workbook **Growth**. Enter your full name in **A1** and your age in **B1**.

2.  Your name has probably been chopped off because it extends beyond the cell boundary. Your age is in cell **B1**. Column **A** needs to be widened.

3.  Position the cursor in the **Column Border**, at the join between two columns, **A** and **B**. The mouse pointer changes to ✚.

    *Click and drag to change the width of column A*

    | A ✚ B | C |
    |---|---|
    | 1 | |
    | 2 | |

4.  Clicking and dragging to the left or right alters the width of the column to the left of the pointer (take care when dragging left, as a width of **0** results in the column being hidden). As the pointer moves, the current column width measurement is displayed next to the cursor, in units and pixels. Drag to the right to widen column **A** until your name is displayed fully.

5.  Click the **Undo** button. To widen a column to fit to the largest entry, place the cursor between **A** and **B** in the column heading as before and **double click**. The column on the left is automatically adjusted to the widest entry in that column.

6.  The longest cell entry is **POPULATION GROWTH (Millions)**, cell **A3**. Reduce the size of column **A** so that it only fits the width of your name.

7.  More than one column can be adjusted at the same time. To adjust several columns, click and drag across the letters in the **Column Border**. Click on **C** and drag across to **D** to select two columns. Adjust either **C** or **D** to a width of **12** units.

8.  Leave the workbook open for the next Driving Lesson.

ℹ️ *There is also a menu option to change **Column Width**, which is **Format | Column | Width**. A number is then entered into the dialog box. Click **OK** to adjust the width.*

# Driving Lesson 70 - Changing Row Height

## ▣ Park and Read

**Row Heights** are increased to create more space between rows of data, making it easier to read the worksheet, or decreased to fit more data on a page.

Row heights are changed in exactly the same way as changing column widths, except the adjust cursor is between two rows and the adjustment changes the row above.

## ⟲ Manoeuvres

1.  Using the workbook **Growth**, point in the **Row Border**, at the division between rows **4** and **5**. The mouse pointer changes to ✛.

2.  The height of each row is **12.75** units. Clicking and dragging up or down now alters the height of the row above (take care when dragging up as a row can be hidden - **0** height). Carefully drag down to make the height of row **4** about **20**.

3.  Select the rows **5** to **12** by dragging in the **Row Border**. Adjust any row by dragging the adjust cursor down to **18**.

4.  Click on any cell to deselect the rows.

5.  Place the cursor between the **6** and **7** in the row border, to display the adjust cursor.

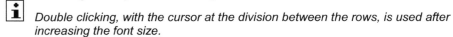

| 5 | Asia | | 478 | 495 | |
| 6 | Africa | | 323 | 448 | |
| 7 | North America | | 212 | 265 | |
| 8 | South America | | 254 | 289 | |
| 9 | Europe | | 424 | 642 | |

6.  Double clicking the adjust cursor between the rows automatically adjusts the row above to the highest entry on that row. Double click and the row height is adjusted to the height of the text on row 6.

ⓘ *Double clicking, with the cursor at the division between the rows, is used after increasing the font size.*

7.  Click the **Undo** button to return row **6** to its previous height.

8.  Leave the workbook open for the next Driving Lesson.

# Driving Lesson 71 - Inserting Rows and Columns

## Park and Read

Rows and columns can be inserted into a worksheet between existing rows and columns when items have been forgotten or new data is to be added.

A problem arises if a worksheet is fully developed with formulas in place. Rows or columns inserted at either end of a range, i.e. the first or last items, will mean an adjustment of all the formulas. **Check all formulas after inserting rows or columns**.

## Manoeuvres

1.  Using the workbook **Growth**, to insert a column between 1975 and 1990 (columns **C** and **D**), click on any cell in column **D**. Select **Insert** and then **Columns**. A new column is inserted to the left of column **D**.

   *New columns are inserted to the left of the active cell and new rows are inserted above it.*

2.  Click **Undo** to reverse the action and use another method. Right click the column border **D** and select **Insert**. A column is inserted.

3.  Click **Undo** to reverse the action. Right click on any cell in column **D**. Select **Insert** and because the column was not selected *Excel* displays the **Insert** dialog box.

4.  Select the **Entire column** option and click **OK**. Rows are inserted in the same way.

5.  Multiple rows and columns can be inserted by selecting the required rows or columns first. To insert 2 rows, click and drag the row numbers **4** and **5** and select **Insert** and then **Rows**. Two new rows are inserted as 4 and 5 above the selected rows.

6.  Leave the workbook open for the next Driving Lesson.

# Driving Lesson 72 - Deleting Rows and Columns

## 🅿 Park and Read

Unwanted extra rows or columns can be deleted.

## 🐎 Manoeuvres

1.    Use the workbook **Growth**.

2.    **Column B** is blank, except for your age and can be removed. Select column **B** by clicking in the column border.

3.    Select **Edit | Delete**. Column **B** is now deleted and replaced by others moving across to the left.

4.    To delete rows **4** and **5**, select the two rows, right click and select **Delete**. Rows 4 and 5 are deleted and the other rows move up to fill the space.

5.    To remove row 2 by another method, place the cursor in any cell on the row and either select **Edit | Delete** or right click and select **Delete**.

6.    Select the required option in the **Delete** dialog box, in this case, **Entire row**. Click on **OK** to delete the row.

7.    Close the workbook <u>without</u> saving.

ℹ️ *The results in cell formulas may be altered by deleting parts of the worksheet, resulting in errors, indicated by #REF in the cells.*

# Driving Lesson 73 - Adding Borders

## Park and Read

Borders are lines around the edges of cells. Border options are available to change the line style, colour and placement of border lines.

## Manoeuvres

1. Open the workbook **Rainfall**. One line has already been added under row 1. This line needs to be thicker.

2. Click cell **A1** and click the down arrow next to the **Borders** button, , on the **Formatting Toolbar** to display the drop down list.

3. There are 12 options available. Select the **Thick Bottom Border** (second line, second button). A thick lines is added under the selected cell.

4. The last chosen option is displayed for future use on the **Borders** button. Highlight the range **B1:E1** and click the **Borders** button to apply the last chosen option, i.e. a thick line.

5. More options are available using the **Format** menu. Highlight the range **A1:E13**, select **Format | Cells** and choose the **Border** tab.

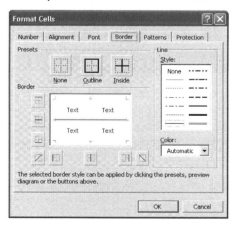

# Driving Lesson 73 - Continued

6.   The grey line across the preview shows that there is a line in the selected range, but not on every cell.

7.   Click twice on the centre line of the preview to remove it. If you have a problem click the **None** button in the **Presets**.

8.   Lines are added to the range of selected cells by clicking the **Presets**, the **Border** buttons or the **Preview** diagram. To add a double line around the outside of the selected cells, click the last option under **Style**, the double line and then click the **Outline** button under **Presets**.

9.   If coloured lines are required, the colour must be selected before adding the lines. To add gridline strength blue lines to the inside of the selected area, click the **Color** drop down and select **blue**.

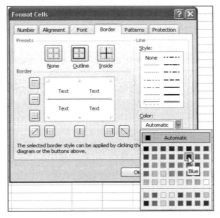

10.   Then select the dotted line style option within the **Line Style** box and then click **Inside**. The **Preview** should look like below.

| Text | Text |
|------|------|
| Text | Text |

11.   Click **OK** to add the lines.

12.   When adding your own lines the gridlines on the worksheet can normally be turned off. Select **Tools | Options**, **View** tab and uncheck **Gridlines** under **Window options**. Click **OK** to return to the worksheet.

13.   Add a thin line to all the cells in the range **A1:E1** (All Borders) using the **Border** button.

[i]   *The **Format Painter**,*  *, can be used for copying borders as well as text, alignment and colour to other cells.*

14.   Print a copy of the worksheet and close it <u>without</u> saving.

# Driving Lesson 74 - Adding Colour

## ▣ Park and Read

Changing the colour of the text is similar to adding bold or italic - it highlights the text and it often looks better. *Excel* calls text colour, **Font Color**.

## ↱ Manoeuvres

1.  Open the workbook **Format**.

2.  On the **Format** sheet, select the range **A2:A16**. Click the **Font Color** button, 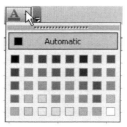. Click away from the range to see that it has changed to the colour shown on the **Font Color** button (**Red** is the default).

3.  Select the same range, **A2:A16** and click the drop down arrow, next to the button to display the colour box.

4.  Select any **Blue** colour. Selecting a colour automatically closes the drop down box and adds that colour to the text in the selected range.

ℹ️ *The **Font Color** can also be changed using **Format |
Cells**, **Font** tab, **Color** box, but it takes longer.*

5.  Highlight the range **B1:N1** and change the text to any colour other than red, blue or black.

ℹ️ *The last colour used will be displayed on the button as the colour for the rest of the current working session. **Red** is displayed as the text colour if the program is restarted.*

6.  As well as changing the colour of the text the cell background can be coloured. Highlight the range **A16:N16** and click the drop down arrow on the **Fill Color** button, . Click on **Light Yellow** to add the background colour.

7.  Fill cell **A1** with a light green. To copy the formatting from this cell, click **Format Painter**, 🖌️.

8.  Click on cell **A16** and notice how the format changes.

9.  To fill the range **B1:N1** with light yellow, select any cell in the range **B16:N16**, then click 🖌️ and click and drag over **B1:N1**.

10. Only if a colour printer is attached, print a copy of the worksheet.

11. Close the workbook <u>without</u> saving.

# Driving Lesson 75 - Rotate Text

## ▣ Park and Read

Text can be displayed vertically or at any angle within a cell.

## ↱ Manoeuvres

1.    Start a new workbook.

2.    In cell **A2** enter **Candidate** and your full name into cell **B2**.

3.    Click on cell **B2** and select **Format | Cells**, **Alignment** tab.

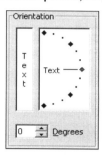

4.    Text is rotated using the **Orientation** section. Click the vertical box with **Text** written in it. Click **OK**. Your name is vertical and the row is increased in height automatically to hold the text.

ℹ️ *If the height of the row had been changed manually previously, then the row height will not change automatically. Adjust the row height manually.*

5.    Click the **Undo** button, [↶ ▾] to return the text to normal.

6.    Display the **Format Cells** dialog box again and use the **Rotation** box on the right to drag the red diamond up to **45** degrees. Click **OK**.

7.    Repeat the last step but drag up to **90** degrees. Click **OK**. Double click the column heading border between **B** and **C** to reduce the width of column to fit the entry. This could be used to create a candidate register or for a form to log assignment results.

8.    Print a copy of the worksheet.

9.    Close the workbook <u>without</u> saving.

# Driving Lesson 76 - Freezing Panes

## Park and Read

**Freeze Panes** is used to keep some rows and/or columns on the screen all the time. This is generally used for labels, while scrolling through a large worksheet. Placement of the active cell is important before freezing as all rows above and all columns to the left are frozen.

## Manoeuvres

1.  Open the workbook **Accounts**. This shows the cash flow of a small hotel.

2.  Before freezing the panes, one question: how much did the hotel pay in **October** for **Wages/NI** (National Insurance)?

3.  Scrolling to the right loses columns at the left and, scrolling down, rows from the top. These important rows/columns on the screen can be frozen. Press <**Ctrl Home**> to return to cell **A1**, then click in cell **B4** (the first cell containing data).

4.  Select **Window | Freeze Panes**. This freezes column **A** and rows **1** to **3**. Find **October's Wages/NI**, by scrolling down and across.

| | A | F | G | H | I | J | K | L | M | N |
|---|---|---|---|---|---|---|---|---|---|---|
| 1 | Accounts for Yea | | | | | | | | | |
| 2 | | | | | | | | | | |
| 3 | Income: | May | June | July | August | September | October | November | December | TOTAL |
| 15 | Payments: | | | | | | | | | |
| 16 | Food | £4,832 | £5,164 | £5,785 | £4,038 | £3,926 | £2,749 | £5,183 | £7,843 | £53,209 |
| 17 | Bar Supplies | £2,394 | £2,786 | £3,164 | £2,067 | £2,262 | £1,863 | £1,673 | £3,082 | £26,945 |
| 18 | Laundry | £604 | £687 | £853 | £634 | £555 | £375 | £274 | £186 | £6,252 |
| 19 | Telecom Charges | £0 | £0 | £1,094 | £0 | £0 | £569 | £0 | £0 | £3,160 |
| 20 | Repairs & Maint. | £1,073 | £857 | £1,146 | £987 | £1,276 | £849 | £654 | £521 | £9,831 |
| 21 | Gas | £0 | £786 | £0 | £0 | £984 | £0 | £0 | £739 | £3,295 |
| 22 | Rates | £0 | £0 | £1,205 | £0 | £0 | £0 | £0 | £0 | £2,410 |
| 23 | Electricity | £1,856 | £0 | £0 | £1,663 | £0 | £0 | £1,205 | £0 | £6,510 |
| 24 | Wages / NI | £5,042 | £5,042 | £6,137 | £6,042 | £5,253 | £4,276 | £4,276 | £5,463 | £60,152 |
| 25 | Insurance | £0 | £1,394 | £0 | £0 | £0 | £0 | £0 | £0 | £3,970 |
| 26 | Administration | £529 | £589 | £634 | £548 | £553 | £429 | £372 | £501 | £5,872 |

*If panes are frozen when a worksheet is saved, they will be still be frozen when the workbook is re-opened.*

5.  When removing the frozen panes, the placing of the active cell is not important. Select the command **Window | Unfreeze Panes**.

6.  Click on cell **A4** and select **Window | Freeze Panes**. This freezes rows 1, 2 and 3 only. Scroll around the worksheet to see the effect.

7.  Select **Window | Unfreeze Panes** to remove the frozen panes.

8.  Click on cell **B1** and select **Window | Freeze Panes**. This freezes column **A** only. Scroll around the worksheet to see the effect.

9.  Select **Window | Unfreeze Panes** to remove the frozen panes.

10. Close the workbook <u>without</u> saving.

# Driving Lesson 77 - Zoom

## 🅿 Park and Read

**Zoom** is used to control the magnification of the worksheet window to see more by making the worksheet smaller, or to see less by making it bigger. The **Zoom** percentage is saved with the worksheet. **Zoom** is purely visual and does not affect the printing of the worksheet.

*ℹ️ This Driving Lesson is affected by the screen resolution. This was prepared on a screen with a 800x600 resolution. More or less of the worksheet may be seen.*

## 🅡 Manoeuvres

1.  Open the workbook **Shop**. This is a worksheet to show the profitability of a small market stall, selling one item.

2.  The **Zoom** box, `100%`, is on the **Standard Toolbar**. This contains a drop down list of several options. Click the down arrow, next to **100%** and select **75%**. The worksheet window is resized to **75%**.

3.  Select each size in turn, except **Selection** to see the effect. Set the **Zoom** percentage to **100%**.

4.  Before the **Selection** option is used, a range to which the zoom is to be applied must be selected. Highlight the range **A1:N1** (the whole width of the worksheet) and select the **Selection** option within **Zoom**.

5.  The **Zoom** box can also be set to any percentage by typing directly into the box. Click the percentage and type **120**, press **<Enter>**.

6.  The same effects can be achieved by using **Zoom** on the **View Menu**. Select **View | Zoom**. This displays the **Zoom** dialog box. Choose **75%** and click **OK**.

7.  Close the workbook <u>without</u> saving.

# Driving Lesson 78 - Revision

This Driving Lesson covers the features introduced in this section. Try not to refer to the preceding Driving Lessons while completing it.

1.   Open the workbook **Balance Sheet**.

2.   The **Balance Sheet 1999** is displayed. To add a centred title, insert two rows at the top of the sheet.

3.   Add the title **Balance Sheet 1999** in **A1**. Change to font size of the title to **16pt** and the merge and centre from **A** to **O**.

4.   Add **Freeze Panes** to keep **Row 1** to **3** and **Columns A & B** on the screen permanently.

5.   Scroll to see the effect of the freeze.

6.   What was the **Shareholders Equity** for **Aug**?

7.   Remove the **Freeze Panes**.

8.   Using the zoom control display the information to fit within the screen.

9.   Change the **Zoom** back to **100%**.

10.   Which year has been the most profitable?

11.   Change the orientation of the page to **Landscape** and **Preview** the worksheet.

12.   Change the print options to fit the worksheet to one piece of paper.

13.   **Preview** the worksheet.

14.   Print one copy of **Balance Sheet 1999**.

15.   Close the workbook <u>without</u> saving the changes.

| i |

*Answers to this revision exercise can be found at the end of this guide.*

If you experienced any difficulty completing this Revision refer back to the Driving Lessons in this section. Then redo the Revision.

# Driving Lesson 79 - Revision

This Driving Lesson covers the features introduced in this section. Try not to refer to the preceding Driving Lessons while completing it.

1. Open the workbook **Apples**.

2. Change the contents of cell **A1** to font size **16pt**.

3. Right align the labels at the top of the columns, including **Total**, i.e. the range **B3:E3**.

4. Change the **Zoom** percentage to **125**.

5. Change the display format for the numbers in the range **B8:E11** to currency with no decimal places, with negative numbers shown in red.

6. Change the width of **Column A** to **12.00** units

7. Widen columns **B** to **E** to **10.00** units.

8. Increase the row height of **Row 3** to **19.50** units.

9. Increase to height of rows **4** to **11** to **15.00** units.

10. Change the vertical alignment of the range **A3:E3** to **Center**.

11. Insert a new column **D** to add **Grapes** to the worksheet. Add the title, **Grapes**. The numbers sold are 0, 1 and 5.

12. Complete the formula to total the new column in **D7**.

13. **Grapes** are bought at **£8** and sold at **£15**. Add this data and the appropriate formulas to cell **D9** and **D11**. What is the **Total Profit** now?

14. Add lines to the inside of the range **A3:F11** and a double line to the outside and remove the gridlines from the screen.

15. Change the colour of the labels to **Blue** and the background colour (**Fill Color** button) to the range **A3:F11** to **Light Yellow**.

16. Print a copy of the worksheet.

17. Save the workbook as **Apples2** and close it.

If you experienced any difficulty completing this Revision refer back to the Driving Lessons in this section. Then redo the Revision.

Once you are confident with the features, complete the Record of Achievement Matrix referring to the section at the end of the guide. Only when competent move on to the next Section.

# Section 9
# Functions &
# Addressing

## By the end of this Section you should be able to:

Use Paste Function

Use the Functions Sum, Count & Average

Use the Functions Max, Min and IF

Use Relative and Absolute Addressing

To gain an understanding of the above features, work through the **Driving Lessons** in this **Section**.

For each **Driving Lesson**, read the **Park and Read** instructions, without touching the keyboard, then work through the numbered steps of the **Manoeuvres** on the computer. Complete the **Revision Exercise(s)** at the end of the section to test your knowledge.

# Driving Lesson 80 - Functions

## 🅿 Park and Read

**Functions** are specialised formulas that make a calculation easier. Just as **Sum** totals a range of cells, other functions such as **Average**, **Min**, **Max** and **Count** can be used to simplify calculations.

Functions can be typed directly into a cell, e.g. **=SUM(A1:B6)** or **Insert Function** can be used to insert the formula structure e.g. **=SUM()**, prior to selecting a range of cells to complete the formula.

## 👉 Manoeuvres

1.  On a new worksheet, enter a column of 10 numbers, starting in **B3**.

2.  Add the numbers by typing **=Sum(B3:B12)** in cell **B13**.

3.  Enter numbers into the cells **D2**, **D3**, **D4** and **D5**. Click on cell **D7**.

4.  Click the **Insert Function** button, 🔖, on the **Formula Bar** to display the **Insert Function** dialog box.

ℹ️ *If the **Office Assistant** is displayed, click **No, don't provide help now**.*

5.  Click on each **Category** in the drop down list to see all available functions.

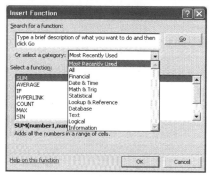

6.  Click the category **Math & Trig** and from **Select a function** select **Sum**. An explanation of the function is given.

7.  Click the **OK** button and a prompt for a range to be summed appears (it may already contain a guess as to the range required). If this box hides the required range, drag it to the right of the screen. Click and drag to select the range **D2:D5**.

8.  Click on **OK**. The function is entered into the worksheet and the result is displayed.

9.  Close the worksheet <u>without</u> saving.

# Driving Lesson 81 - Count

## ▣ Park and Read

The function **COUNT** counts the cells that contain numbers in a range. **COUNTA** counts the number of cells that are <u>not</u> empty and **COUNTBLANK** counts empty cells in a range.

## ↱ Manoeuvres

1.  Open the workbook **Marks**. This shows the exam results for one pupil, **Ali Kazan**. The task is to add the calculations in the form of functions to be able to rate the candidate's performance.

2.  Click on cell **E7** and click the **Insert Function** button, 🔳.

3.  Click on **Statistical** in the **Select a category** list and then select **COUNT** in the **Select a function** list.

4.  Click **OK** to display the **Function Arguments** box. Move the dialog box to the right, if necessary.

5.  Select the range **B4:B21** (the cells that might contain numbers).

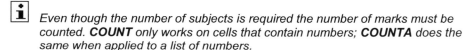

*Even though the number of subjects is required the number of marks must be counted. **COUNT** only works on cells that contain numbers; **COUNTA** does the same when applied to a list of numbers.*

6.  Click **OK** to complete the function.

7.  **Ali** failed to turn up for the German exam. Enter **0** in cell **B8**. The number of subjects now shows one more as **Zero** counts as a number.

8.  Delete the function in cell **E7**.

9.  Click **Insert Function**, 🔳, again and this time select **COUNTBLANK** from **Statistical**.

10. Select the range **B4:B21** and click **OK**.

11. Notice how the number of blank cells has been counted.

12. Delete this function and replace it with the original **COUNT** function.

13. Leave the workbook open for the next Driving Lesson.

# Driving Lesson 82 - Average and Round

## 🅿 Park and Read

**Average** adds a list of numbers and divides by the number of numbers.

Sometimes it is required to show numerical data to a specific level of precision, for example to show a price field to the nearest pound or an age to the nearest year. To do this: either use formatting (which does not change the actual content) or use the **Round** function.

## ☞ Manoeuvres

1.  The workbook **Marks** should be open from the last exercise, if not open it.

2.  Click in cell **E8**. Click the **Insert Function** button, 🔲. Click on **Statistical** in the **Function category** list and select **AVERAGE** in the **Select a Function** list.

3.  Click **OK** to display the **Function Arguments** box for **AVERAGE**. Drag it to the right of the screen, away from the marks.

4.  Select the range **B4:B21** (the cells that might contain numbers, the box collapses and on release of the mouse expands again). Click **OK** to complete the function.

5.  The **0** for **German** is reducing the average as it is counted as a numeric cell. It is decided that **Ali** should not have been registered for **German**, delete the zero in cell **B8**. The **Average** mark increases.

6.  With the workbook **Marks** open, start a new workbook. In cell **B3** enter **27.32** and in cell **B4** enter **27.68**.

7.  Highlight **B3:B4** and use **Format | Cells** to format the range as **Number** with **0** decimal places. Click **OK**. The numbers are displayed to the nearest whole number. The cell content has not been changed, only the appearance. **B4** displays **28** in the cell. Click on **B4**. The **Formula Bar** still shows the cell content as **27.68**.

8.  Undo the formatting and in **C3** enter the formula **=B3*1.15** to calculate the new value for **B3** after a 15% increase. Copy the formula down to **C4**.

9.  In **D3** enter the formula **=ROUND(C3,0)**. This rounds the value in **C3** to have **0** decimal places. Copy the formula down to **D4**. The values are shown as whole numbers.

ℹ️ *The **Round** function could have been applied directly with the calculation as =ROUND((B3\*1.15),0). This would calculate the new value and apply the rounding in one formula.*

10. Close the workbook <u>without</u> saving, but leave the workbook **Marks** open.

# Driving Lesson 83 - Maximum and Minimum

## Park and Read

**MAX**    the function for maximum, finds and displays the largest number in the selected range.

**MIN**    the function for minimum, finds and displays the smallest number in the selected range.

## Manoeuvres

1.    The workbook **Marks** should still be open. If not, open it.

2.    Enter the text **Highest Mark** in cell **D9** and **Lowest Mark** in cell **D10**.

3.    Click in cell **E9**. Click the **Insert Function** button, 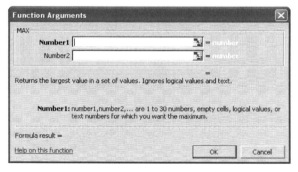.

4.    Click on **Statistical** in the **Function category** list and select **MAX** in the **Select a Function** list.

5.    Click **OK** to display the **MAX** box.

6.    Click the **Collapse** button, 🖳, at the right side of the **Number1** box.

7.    Select the same range as before **B4:B21**.

8.    Click the **Expand** button, 🖃, in the box and click **OK** to complete the function. The highest mark is **95**.

9.    In cell **E10** enter the **MIN** function using the same range to display the lowest mark.

10.   To test the four functions created, change the marks in **B17** to **50** and **B6** to **83** and note the changes in the function values.

11.   Save the workbook as **Marks2** and then close it.

# Driving Lesson 84 - IF

## 🅿 Park and Read

The logical function **IF** compares the contents of a cell and, if a logical test is met, performs one action; if not, it performs another.

**=IF(Logical_test,Value_if_true,Value_if_false)**

For instance, if the value in cell **A1** is greater than 10 then multiply it by 3, if not, multiply it by 2. This is expressed as: **=IF(A1>10,A1*3,A1*2)**

The **IF** function is sometimes described as **IF THEN ELSE**. **IF** the condition is true **THEN** do this **ELSE** do that. The parts are separated by commas.

## Manoeuvres

1.  On a blank worksheet, enter the labels **Interest Calculation** in **B1**, **Balance** in cell **B3** and **Interest** in cell **B4**.

2.  Enter **200** in **C3** for your bank balance.

3.  The interest on your money depends on whether the balance is over or under £**100**. Click in cell **C4**, click the **Insert Function** button, 🔣. Select **IF** from the **Logical** category.

4.  Click **OK** and enter the following parts of the test with a mixture of pointing at cell references and typing.

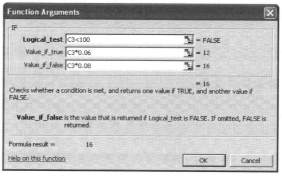

5.  Click **OK** to complete the function. The function looks at the value of cell **C3** and if it is less than **100**, calculates the interest at **6%** of the value, otherwise it calculates it at **8%**.

6.  The result of the function, the interest, depends on the balance. Move to **C3** and enter **1000**. The interest is £**80**, the higher rate (8%). Enter **50** and the interest is £**3** (6%). Experiment, change the balance and see the interest change. The **IF** function is very powerful.

7.  Close the workbook <u>without</u> saving.

# Driving Lesson 85 - Relative Addressing

## ▣ Park and Read

As a formula is copied to a new location, by default the cell references in the formula change automatically. The new calculation is performed on cells in the same positions relative to the original formula, e.g. references to **B2+B3** become **C2+C3** then **D2+D3**, as the formula is copied to the right from column to column. This is Relative Addressing.

## ↱ Manoeuvres

1.    Start a new workbook.

2.    In **B2** enter **7** and **B3** enter **8**.

3.    Select cell **B4** and click the **AutoSum** button, $\boxed{\Sigma \; \cdot}$, to add the contents of the two cells above. Press <**Enter**> to accept the range and perform the calculation. The answer should be **15** and the formula **=SUM(B2:B3)**.

4.    Use the **Fill Handle** to copy this formula across to cell **C4**. The displayed answer is **0** because the two cells above are empty. Click on cell **C4** to display the formula, it is **=SUM(C2:C3)**. It sums the two cells directly above.

5.    Enter **3** in cell **C2** and **5** in cell **C3**. The answer in cell **C4** is **8**.

6.    Copy cell **B4** to cell **E8**. What is the formula in cell **E8**?

7.    Enter any two numbers in the cells **E6** and **E7** to test the formula.

8.    Close the workbook <u>without</u> saving.

9.    Open the workbook **Accounts**. This is basic cash flow (the flow of money in and out) for a small hotel.

10.   Click on cell **B14**. This sums the cash coming into the hotel for **January** (**Turnover**).

11.   Use any method to copy this formula to the range **C14:N14**.

12.   Click on cell **E14** (the turnover for **April**). It sums the same range of rows as in cell **B14**, except using the cells in column **E**.

13.   Close the workbook <u>without</u> saving.

ℹ️ *Answers to this exercise can be found at the end of this guide.*

# Driving Lesson 86 - Absolute Addressing

## **P** Park and Read

**Absolute** addressing is used when the same cell is to be used even when copying formulas. When formulas use the same cell, it is easy to make changes to all the formulas.

The **Absolute** reference key is the **$** sign. **D7** is a **Relative** address that will change if the formula is copied and **$D$7** is an **Absolute** address that will stay the same. The dollars fix the cell so that it copies without changing.

## Manoeuvres

1. Open the workbook **World Population**. This workbook contains some population statistics.

2. The population of Europe in 1975 was **424** million. The world population was **1953** million. Click on cell **C8**, Europe's population as a percentage of the world. Note the formula **=B8/$B$11**. The cell **B11** has been made **Absolute** and does not change in the formulas in column **C**.

3. Close the workbook <u>without</u> saving.

4. Open the workbook **Absolute**.

5. The average mark is calculated in cell **B23** as **63**. Click in cell **B23** and view the formula (the **Average** function).

6. To compare each mark with the average, click in cell **C4** and enter the formula **=B4-B23** using any method. The answer is **2** (65 is 2 marks above the average of 63).

7. If the formula is left as **Relative**, the other cells will not work. Copy the formula in cell **C4** to cell **C5**. The formula is **=B5-B24** the cells have moved down one row. **B24** is empty, therefore the answer is **55**.

8. Delete the contents of cell **C5**. Click in cell **C4**. The cell reference **B23** needs to be fixed, i.e. made **Absolute**. Change **B23** to **$B$23**.

9. Use the **Fill Handle** or any other method to copy cell **C4** down the range **C5:C21**. The average mark **63** is used in all the formulas in column **C**.

10. Change the **English Literature** mark to **72**.

**i** *All the cells in the range **C4:C21** have changed because **B23** has changed.*

11. Close the workbook <u>without</u> saving.

# Driving Lesson 87 - Revision

This Driving Lesson covers the features introduced in this section. Try not to refer to the preceding Driving Lessons while completing it.

1.   What name is given to cell references in a formula which change when the formula is copied to a new location?

2.   What symbol is used to show that references are **Absolute**?

3.   If a formula in a cell is **=C2+$E$5** what would the formula be if this was copied   a) down one cell?   b) to the right one cell?

4.   If you copied the formula **=B3+D4** in **C6** to cell **F8**, what would the formula be in cell **F8**? You can create this on a worksheet if it helps.

5.   When would you use **Absolute Addressing**?

6.   Start a new workbook and create the worksheet below.

|   | A | B | C | D | E |
|---|---|---|---|---|---|
| 1 |   |   |   |   |   |
| 2 |   |   |   |   |   |
| 3 |   | Number Sold |   | 20 |   |
| 4 |   | Buying Price |   | 5 |   |
| 5 |   | Selling Price |   | 6 |   |
| 6 |   | Profit |   |   |   |
| 7 |   |   |   |   |   |

7.   The reason for using column **D** for the numbers is that the text is too long for column **B**. It spilled over into column **C**. Widen column **B** to hold all the text.

8.   Delete column **C**.

9.   Calculate the **Profit** in **C6** (remember brackets).

10.  Change the **Number Sold** to **534**, the **Buying Price** to **2.56** and the **Selling Price** to **3.99**.

11.  Format cell **C6** to display currency with two decimal places.

12.  How much is the **Profit**?

13.  Close the workbook <u>without</u> saving.

ℹ️  *Answers to this revision exercise can be found at the end of this guide.*

If you experienced any difficulty completing this Revision refer back to the Driving Lessons in this section. Then redo the Revision.

# Driving Lesson 88 - Revision

This Driving Lesson covers the features introduced in this section. Try not to refer to the preceding Driving Lessons while completing it.

1.  The following data represents sales figures for a group of salespersons. Construct the spreadsheet and add the data at the positions shown.

| | A | B | C | D |
|---|---|---|---|---|
| 1 | Analysis of Sales Figures | | | |
| 2 | | | | |
| 3 | Salesperson | Sales | Average +/- | |
| 4 | Smith | 1300 | | |
| 5 | Brown | 8965 | | |
| 6 | Bloggs | 21050 | | |
| 7 | White | 17800 | | |
| 8 | Green | | | |
| 9 | Chapman | 670 | | |
| 10 | Hall | 1809 | | |
| 11 | | | | |
| 12 | Total | | | |
| 13 | Average Sales | | | |
| 14 | No of Salespersons | | | |
| 15 | Lowest Sales | | | |
| 16 | Highest Sales | | | |
| 17 | | | | |

2.  Enter the functions for **Total** and **Average Sales** in **B12** and **B13**.

3.  The number of salespersons is calculated using the **COUNT** function (Remember to count the sales figures, not the salespersons' names).

4.  The high and low sales use **MAX** and **MIN**. Similar to **Count** but display the largest and smallest. They can be found in **Statistical**.

5.  The **Average +/-** column is to be the variation of an individual's sales compared to the average, calculated by subtracting the average sales value from the individual's sales. For **C4** this is **=B4-B13** (Remember **Absolute** and **Relative** addressing if copying formulas down the column).

6.  Print a copy of the worksheet.

7.  Save the workbook as **Sales** then close it.

| i |
|---|

*It is very important to decide whether to put a zero in cell **B8** or to leave it blank. Try it! The answers will be different.*

If you experienced any difficulty completing this Revision refer back to the Driving Lessons in this section. Then redo the Revision.

Once you are confident with the features, complete the Record of Achievement Matrix referring to the section at the end of the guide. Only when competent move on to the next Section.

# Section 10
# Charts

## By the end of this Section you should be able to:

**Create a Chart**

**Create an Embedded Chart**

**Select Chart Type**

**Move, Copy and Resize Charts**

**Format a Chart**

**Print Charts**

**Use Chart Options**

To gain an understanding of the above features, work through the **Driving Lessons** in this **Section**.

For each **Driving Lesson**, read the **Park and Read** instructions, without touching the keyboard, then work through the numbered steps of the **Manoeuvres** on the computer. Complete the **Revision Exercise(s)** at the end of the section to test your knowledge.

# Driving Lesson 89 - Introducing Charts

## Park and Read

It can be difficult to find vital information like changes in trends or performance from rows and columns of numeric data.  A picture of the figures, **a graph or chart**, helps to identify subtle changes that may have otherwise been missed. Some of the standard chart types available are:

| | | |
|---|---|---|
| **Column** | - | Shaded vertical columns |
| **Bar** | - | Shaded horizontal bars |
| **Line** | - | Points connected by a line |
| **Pie** | - | Data as slices of a circular pie |

There are also various 3-D versions and different versions of the same chart type.

There are two ways in which charts can be created: as part of a worksheet, appearing on the sheet, with the data (an **Embedded** chart) or as a completely separate sheet, **Chart1**.

## Manoeuvres

1.    Open the workbook **Charts**. This workbook contains both an embedded chart and charts created on separate sheets.

2.    Click the **London Rainfall** sheet. This is a chart that has been created on a separate sheet.

3.    Click the **Data** sheet. This sheet contains the source information used for the charts. Scroll down the worksheet to see the embedded chart under the data.

4.    Click the **Bombay Rainfall** sheet. This is a chart similar to the **London Rainfall** on a separate sheet.

5.    Close the workbook **Charts** <u>without</u> saving.

# Driving Lesson 90 - Creating Charts

## P Park and Read

Charts are created using the **Chart Wizard**. It consists of four steps as follows:

| | | |
|---|---|---|
| Chart Type | - | Select the type and subtype |
| Source Data | - | Select the Data Range on the worksheet to be charted |
| Chart Options | - | Select the Titles, Legends, Labels, etc. |
| Chart Location | - | As new sheet or as an object in a named sheet |

## Manoeuvres

1. Open the workbook **Rainfall**. This workbook contains the average rainfall for four major cities in the world. Charts are to be created to show this information.

2. When creating a chart the data can either be highlighted before starting, or within a step in the **Chart Wizard**. If it is highlighted first then the results can be previewed. To chart **London's** rainfall, select the range **A1:B13** (this is the rainfall and the labels).

3. Either select **Insert | Chart** or click the **Chart Wizard** button, . The **Chart Wizard** starts at **Step 1 of 4 - Chart Type**.

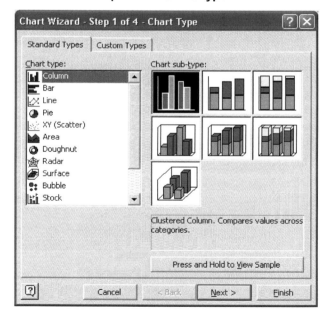

# Driving Lesson 90 - Continued

4.  **Column** is the selected **Chart type**, the **Chart sub-types** are shown on the right. Select the first on the second row (**Clustered column with a 3-D visual effect**). Press and hold down the mouse button on the **Press and Hold to View Sample** button.

5.  Click **Next**. Step **2** of the wizard is the **Chart Source Data**, the data has already been selected. Click **Next**.

6.  Step **3** of the wizard is the **Chart Options**. Click on each of the 6 tabs in turn to see the available options.

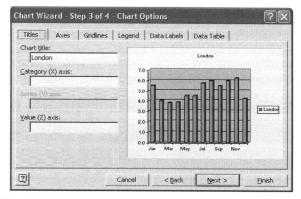

7.  Click back on **Titles**. Type **Rainfall (cm)** under **Value (Z) axis**.

8.  Click the **Legend** tab (Legends show which columns belong to which data series). There is only one set of data, so uncheck **Show legend**. Click **Next**.

9.  **Step 4 of 4** is **Chart Location**.

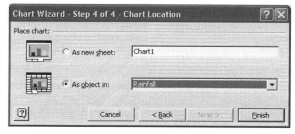

10. Select the **As new sheet** and enter the sheet name **London Rainfall** as a replacement for **Chart1**. Click **Finish** to create the chart.

11. Save the workbook as **Rainfall2** and leave the workbook open for the next Driving Lesson.

# Driving Lesson 91 - Embedded Charts

## ▣ Park and Read

As well as creating charts on a sheet by themselves, they can be placed on the same sheet as the data. This is called an **Embedded Chart**. When complete, the chart is placed on the worksheet and can be moved, resized or deleted.

## ⌔ Manoeuvres

1.  The workbook **Rainfall2** should still be open, if not, open it.

2.  Select the sheet **Rainfall**. An embedded chart of the rainfall in **Bombay** is going to be created.

3.  Two separate ranges need to be selected to chart **Bombay's** rainfall, the labels and the actual rainfall data. Select **A1:A13** and hold <Ctrl> down while selecting the other range **C1:C13**.

| | A | B | C | D | E | F |
|---|---|---|---|---|---|---|
| 1 | RAINFALL(cms) | London | Bombay | Adelaide | Tokyo | |
| 2 | Jan | 5.5 | 0.5 | 1.8 | 5.0 | |
| 3 | Feb | 4.0 | 0.5 | 1.8 | 7.0 | |
| 4 | Mar | 3.8 | 0.0 | 2.5 | 10.0 | |
| 5 | Apr | 3.9 | 0.0 | 4.0 | 14.0 | |
| 6 | May | 4.5 | 2.0 | 7.0 | 13.0 | |
| 7 | Jun | 4.5 | 24.0 | 8.0 | 18.0 | |
| 8 | Jul | 5.8 | 24.0 | 7.0 | 14.0 | |
| 9 | Aug | 6.0 | 24.0 | 6.0 | 14.0 | |
| 10 | Sep | 5.5 | 24.0 | 5.0 | 21.0 | |
| 11 | Oct | 6.0 | 4.5 | 4.5 | 22.0 | |
| 12 | Nov | 6.3 | 1.0 | 3.0 | 10.0 | |
| 13 | Dec | 4.3 | 0.0 | 2.5 | 6.0 | |
| 14 | | | | | | |

4.  Click the **Chart Wizard** button, 📊, to start creating the chart. The creation of the chart is exactly the same as in the previous Driving Lesson. Make the same choices for steps 1 to 3 of the wizard (title **Bombay Rainfall**).

5.  At step 4 of the wizard the option **As object in** and the sheet **Rainfall** are already selected. Click **Finish**. The chart is placed over the data on the sheet.

6.  The chart can be moved by clicking and dragging. You need to select the chart first; click the **Chart Area**. Drag it below the data.

7.  To resize the chart, click and drag on the black handles around it. Click the black handle in the centre on the right and drag to the right to make the chart wider, till all the months are displayed on the chart horizontally. Any handle can be used to resize.

ℹ️ *To delete an embedded chart, click on it to select it and press the <**Delete**> key.*

8.  Save the workbook using the same name and close it.

# Driving Lesson 92 - Chart Types

## 🅿 Park and Read

Different types of chart are used for different data. The most common type of chart is a **Column** chart as seen already. It displays the data in columns and is used to compare values. **Bar** charts are column charts where the values are horizontal bars and not vertical columns. **Line** charts are used to display the movement of values as with sales or profits from over time. **Pie** charts display the values as slices of circle. The size of each slice represents the value of the data on which it is based, as a fraction of the total. Pie charts are used to show values as a part of the whole as with product costs or expenditure.

## ☞ Manoeuvres

1.  Open the workbook **Computer Data**. Four different types of chart are to be created using the same data to show the different representations of each.

2.  Highlight the data in the cells **A3:B8** (include the titles but not the totals, as they are rarely included in charts).

3.  Click the **Chart Wizard** button, 📊 and from the **Chart type** list, select the option, 🔘 Pie .

4.  From the **Chart sub-type** area, choose the first option, a basic pie chart and click **Next**.

5.  The dialog box displays the **Chart Source Data**, the data to be used has already been selected, click **Next**.

6.  The third dialog box allows the **Chart Options** to be changed, the **Chart title**, **Computer Sales** should be entered automatically. Click **Next**.

7.  The final step allows the location of the pie chart to be selected. Select the **As new sheet** option and enter the name, **Pie Chart**.

8.  Click **Finish**. The **Pie Chart** is created on its own sheet next to **Data**.

9.  Return to the **Data** sheet and using the same range, create a **Column** chart with the default sub-type on a new sheet named **Column Chart**.

10. Repeat the last step to create a **Bar Chart** and then again to create a **Line Chart**. The sheet tabs should be as in the diagram:

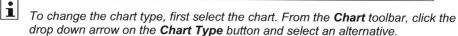

ℹ️ *To change the chart type, first select the chart. From the **Chart** toolbar, click the drop down arrow on the **Chart Type** button and select an alternative.*

11. Leave the workbook open for the next Driving Lesson.

# Driving Lesson 93 - Copy, Move & Resize Charts

## ▣ Park and Read

Charts can be copied, resized and deleted.

## ↷ Manoeuvres

1. The **Computer Data** workbook should still be open, if not, open it.

2. To copy a chart from one sheet to another, click on the **Bar Chart** sheet tab. Move around the chart and when the **Chart Area** tooltip is displayed, click to select the whole chart.

3. Click the **Copy** button, 🖹 or press <**Ctrl C**>.

4. To copy the chart to the **Data** sheet, display it, select cell **A11** and then click the **Paste** button, 🖹▾, or press <**Ctrl V**> to paste the chart on to the **Data** sheet.

5. The chart is too big. Drag a corner handle towards the centre of the chart to reduce its size until the whole chart fits on the screen.

6. Charts can be copied from workbook to workbook. Copy the **Line Chart** and start a new workbook. Paste the chart on to **Sheet1**.

7. If the chart is required on a separate sheet and not embedded as it is now, with the chart highlighted, select **Chart | Location** and select the **As new sheet** option, name the sheet as **Line Chart** and click **OK**.

ℹ️ *Embedded charts are moved from book to book using **Cut**, ✂ or <**Ctrl X**> and* **Paste**, 🖹▾ *or press <**Ctrl V**>, the same method used for moving a range. Charts on separate sheets are moved from book to book using the same method as moving a normal worksheet, see Section 5.*

8. Close the new workbook <u>without</u> saving.

9. Display the **Data** sheet of the **Computer Data** workbook.

10. Click the bar chart to select it and then click 🖹 or press <**Ctrl C**>. Place the active cell beneath the chart and click 🖹▾ or press <**Ctrl V**> to create a copy of the chart.

11. To delete the second, embedded chart, click the chart to display its handles and then press <**Delete**>. The embedded chart is removed.

12. Delete the first bar chart.

13. Save the workbook as **Computer Data2** and leave it open.

# Driving Lesson 94 - Formatting Charts

## P Park and Read

All parts of a chart, including the colours, axes, text, gridlines, chart and plot area, can be changed.

## Manoeuvres

1.  The workbook **Computer Data2** should still be open, if not open it.

2.  Select the **Bar Chart** sheet tab. Place the mouse cursor on different parts of the chart and read the **ToolTips**.

3.  Click the chart title **Computer Sales** and press <**Delete**> to remove it.

4.  Any and every part of a chart can be changed by formatting. Point at the grey background, the **Plot Area** and double click. The **Format Plot Area** dialog box is displayed.

5.  It has a **Patterns** tab. This deals with the **Border** around the title and the **Area** (background colour). Select a light yellow **Area** colour and click **OK**.

**i** *The colour of the background to a chart is more important if viewed on screen. Printed charts can have the **Plot Area** set to none to save ink or toner.*

6.  Click the **Column Chart** sheet to make it active.

7.  To change the colour of the columns, point at any column and then double click to display the **Format Data Series** dialog box.

**i** *Any part of a chart can be double clicked to display the **Format** box for that item. Only the options that can be changed will be available.*

8.  Make sure the **Patterns** tab is selected. From **Area** select **Red** as a colour for all the columns; the **sample** box shows what it will look like. Click **OK**.

9.  The colour of a single data point can also be changed. To change the Sunderland column to blue, the correct column has to be selected. Click away from the columns. Click the **Sunderland** column (to select the entire series) and click again to select the single data point (handles are displayed around it). Either double click the selected column or select **Format | Selected Data Point**.

10. Select **Blue** under **Area** and click **OK**.

11. Display the **Pie Chart** and using the same technique change the colour of the **Sunderland** slice to **Blue**. Click **OK**.

12. A feature specific to **Pie Charts** is the ability to explode all or a single slice. With the **Sunderland** slice selected, click and drag outwards slightly from the centre, release the mouse to drop the slice; this slice is now highlighted to draw attention to it.

13. Save the workbook using the same name and leave it open.

# Driving Lesson 95 - Chart Options

## 🅿 Park and Read

To make any changes to a chart, the chart or specific part of the chart has to be selected by clicking on the relevant part first. This displays the **Chart** menu from which **Chart Options** can be selected.

All parts of a chart, including the titles, legend, data labels and chart type can be changed. Text boxes can also be added to include supporting information.

## 🔃 Manoeuvres

1.  The workbook **Computer Data2** should still be open, if not open it.

2.  Text can be added to charts via text boxes. If the **Drawing** toolbar is not displayed, (usually along the lower edge of the screen), select **View | Toolbars** and click **Drawing**.

3.  Click the **Text Box** button, 🔲, on the **Drawing** toolbar and then click and drag a rectangle in the centre of the **Sunderland** slice. On releasing the mouse the cursor is placed in the box, type **Sunderland** and click away from the box when complete. A text box is moved by dragging its border.

4.  Click once on the text box, to select its contents, it will show a border. The text can now be changed and formatted. Highlight the word **Sunderland**, increase the font size to **14** and make it *italic*. The size of the text box may need increasing. Click away from the box to deselect it.

5.  Any text on a chart, i.e. title, axes, legend text, can all be changed in the same way - try it.

6.  To delete a text box, click it once then click again on the box border. The pattern of the border will change. Press <**Delete**>. Delete the **Sunderland** label from the **Pie Chart** in this way.

7.  Data labels can be displayed on the chart. Select **Chart | Chart Options** and the **Data Labels** tab. From **Label Contents**, check the **Category name** and **Value** options and click **OK**.

8.  Instead of displaying values, percentages can be shown on a pie chart. Select **Chart | Chart Options** again and in **Label Contents** click to remove the check next to **Value** and check **Percentage**. Click **OK**. The displays the percentage next to each segment.

9.  Display the **Bar Chart**.

10. Right click on the **Legend** and select **Format Legend**. On the **Patterns** tab, choose a pale colour from the **Area** section. Click **OK** and the legend is filled with colour.

# Driving Lesson 95 - Continued

11. To add a title to a chart, select **Chart | Chart Options**. This dialog box controls many of the chart features. With the **Titles** tab active, enter **Computer Sales 2002** as the title.

12. With **Chart Options** still displayed, click on the **Legend** tab and remove the legend by clicking on **Show legend** to uncheck it. Click **OK** to apply the two changes.

13. The type of chart can be changed after completion. With the **Bar Chart** still displayed, select **Chart | Chart Type** and step 1 of the **Chart Wizard** is displayed. With **Bar** still selected as the main type, select **Clustered bar with a 3-D visual effect**. Click **OK**.

**i**    *Any chart object can be changed in a similar way.*

14. Make the **Line Chart** active. To change the colour of the line double click on it to display the **Format Data Series** dialog box. Under **Line** using the **Color** drop down list, select **red** as the line colour. Increase the thickness of the line using the drop down list in the **Weight** box. Click **OK** to confirm the change.

15. Save the workbook using the same name and leave it open.

# Driving Lesson 96 - Printing Charts

## ▣ Park and Read

**Charts** created on a new worksheet are printed as a normal worksheet, via the **Print** button or the **File | Print** command.

**Embedded charts** can be printed with the rest of the sheet using the commands already stated. An embedded chart can be printed by itself by selecting it before displaying the **Print** dialog box.

## ⌒ Manoeuvres

1.  The workbook **Computer Data2** should still be open. If not open it.

2.  To print the **Column Chart**, display the correct sheet. Double click the **Plot Area** and remove the background colour by selecting **None** and clicking **OK**.

3.  Select **File | Print** or press **<Ctrl P>** and click **OK**. A single copy of the chart is printed using the default settings.

4.  A quicker way to print any worksheet using the default settings is to use the **Print** button. Click the **Pie Chart** tab and then click the **Print** button, . A single copy of the chart is printed.

5.  Click the **Data** sheet, highlight the range **A3:B8**, click the **Chart Wizard** button,  and proceed to create an embedded **Column Chart** as an object in the **Data** sheet. Move the chart away from the data.

6.  Click away from the chart to de-select it.

7.  Click on the chart to select it (handles are displayed on the object) select **File | Print**. The **Print** dialog box shows **Selected Chart** as the chosen option. Click **OK** to print just the chart.

ℹ️ *Embedded charts are seldom printed by themselves as the quality is always of a poorer standard. Resizing does not help.*

8.  Resize the chart to display all the column labels. Print a copy of the chart and compare with the previous one.

9.  Click away from the embedded chart on any cell and select **File | Print** the **Print** dialog box displays **Active sheet(s)** as the default option. Click **OK** to print a copy of the whole worksheet including the chart.

10. Save the workbook as **Computer Data2**, the same file name.

11. Close the workbook.

# Driving Lesson 97 - Revision

This Driving Lesson covers the features introduced in this section. Try not to refer to the preceding Driving Lessons while completing it.

1. What is used to create a chart in *Excel*?

2. How is this feature started?

3. Would you select the source data before or after starting to create a chart? Why?

4. Name the three most commonly used types of chart.

5. Name the other chart types.

6. If you were given the weekly sales figures for a company, what type of chart would you create to best demonstrate the data?

7. What type of chart would you create to represent the breakdown of costs involved with producing a particular product?

8. A **Bar Chart** and a **Column Chart** are similar, but what is the difference?

*Answers to this revision exercise can be found at the end of this guide.*

If you experienced any difficulty completing this Revision refer back to the Driving Lessons in this section. Then redo the Revision.

# Driving Lesson 98 - Revision

This Driving Lesson covers the features introduced in this section. Try not to refer to the preceding Driving Lessons while completing it.

1.  Open the workbook **Analysis**.

2.  Create a 2D pie chart on a new worksheet to be called **Sales Chart**, using the range **A3:B10**. At step 3 of the **Wizard**, add the chart title **Sales Analysis Figures**, show a **Legend** and apply **Data Labels** to show **Value**.

3.  Draw a text box over each segment and type in the appropriate name. Change the **Font** colour so the names can be easily read. Move each text box to a central position in the sector.

4.  Format the title to be **16** point and **Blue** text.

5.  Remove the **Legends** and print a copy

6.  The final chart should look as below.

### Sales Analysis Figures

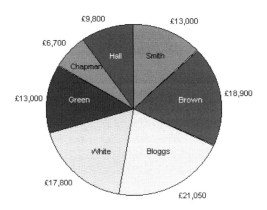

7.  Close the workbook <u>without</u> saving.

If you experienced any difficulty completing this Revision refer back to the Driving Lessons in this section. Then redo the Revision.

Once you are confident with the features, complete the Record of Achievement Matrix referring to the section at the end of the guide.

# Answers

## Driving Lesson 11

Step 2     By a heavy border and the cell reference is displayed in the **Formula Bar**

Step 3     There are **3** by default - **Sheet1**, **Sheet2** and **Sheet3**

Step 4     a) **Save**, b) **Print** (and the name of the printer), c) **New**, d) **Open**

Step 5     **18**

Step 6     **5** or **7**. **Paste** and **Paste Special** will not be ghosted if any copying has been carried out since starting the computer.

## Driving Lesson 12

Step 2     **<End>** →

Step 3     **65536**

Step 4     **<Ctrl Home>**

## Driving Lesson 16

Step 7     The workbook **Budget** is active as it has just been opened.

## Driving Lesson 31

Step 2     Column

Step 3     42

Step 4     21

Step 7     37

## Driving Lesson 50

Step 4     £208

Step 7     £170

Step 9     £80

## Driving Lesson 51

Step 4     **Friday** and 2003 was **not** a leap year

Step 10     **23725** days old at age 65 (approximately).

## Driving Lesson 78

Step 6     £9876

Step 10     1999

# Answers

## Driving Lesson 79

Step 13 £388

## Driving Lesson 85

Step 6    **=SUM(E6:E7)**

## Driving Lesson 87

Step 1    **Relative Addressing**

Step 2    **$**

Step 3    a) **=C3+$E$5**   b) **=D2+$E$5**

Step 4    **=E5+G6**

Step 5    When one cell contains information to be used by formulas in several locations.

Step 12 £763.62

## Driving Lesson 97

Step 1    **Chart Wizard**

Step 2    Selecting **Insert | Chart** or with the **Chart Wizard** button, .

Step 3    Can be done either way, but before if possible, to be able to preview.

Step 4    **Column**, **Line** and **Pie**

Step 5    **Bar**, **XY Scatter**, **Area**, **Doughnut**, **Radar**, **Surface**, **Bubble**, **Stock**, **Cylinder**, **Cone** and **Pyramid**.

Step 6    **Line** or **Column** chart

Step 7    **Pie** chart

Step 8    **Column** chart the data is represented by vertical columns and a **Bar** chart displays horizontal bars. The two axes change places.

# Glossary

| | |
|---|---|
| **Addressing** | A method of referencing cells, relative or absolute |
| **Alignment** | The position of data in a cell |
| **AutoSum** | A function to sum a range of numbers |
| **Average** | Function that adds a range and divides the number of numbers |
| **Border** | The edge of a cell, type and colour of line |
| **Chart** | A pictorial representation of data |
| **Count** | Function that displays the number of numbers in a range |
| **Embedded Chart** | A chart placed on a standard worksheet, usually with the source data |
| **Excel** | Spreadsheet software |
| **Fill Handle** | A cursor used to copy data |
| **Font** | A type or style of text |
| **Footer** | Information appearing on the bottom of every page |
| **Format** | Changing the appearance of information |
| **Formula** | A calculation, can use values and/or cell references |
| **Freeze Panes** | Fixing information on screen so that it is not affected by scrolling |
| **Function** | Specialised formulas that make calculations easier |
| **Header** | Information appearing on the top of every page |
| **HTML** | A format that can be read over the Internet (**H**yper**T**ext **M**arkup **L**anguage) |
| **IF** | Logical function that a carries out a test and performs one action if true and another if false |
| **Maximum** | Function that displays the largest number in a range |
| **Minimum** | Function that displays the smallest number in a range |
| **Office Assistant** | An on-screen help system |
| **Pixel** | Small squares that make up the screen, normally 800 by 600 |
| **Preferences** | Customisation of basic options |
| **Range** | A group of adjacent cells |
| **Workbook** | A spreadsheet file |
| **Worksheet** | A single page within a workbook |
| **Zoom** | Worksheet magnification on-screen only |

# Index

**Addressing**
  Absolute 119
  Relative 118

**Alignment 98**

**AutoSum 45**

**Average 115**

**Bold 93**

**Borders 104**

**Brackets 44**

**Calculations**
  Brackets 44
  Formulas 43

**Cells**
  Copying 67
  Formatting 92
  Merge 99
  Moving 69

**Charts 122**
  Copy, Move and Resize 128
  Creating 124
  Embedded 126
  Formatting 129
  Introduction 123
  Options 130
  Printing 132
  Types 127

**Clipboard 67**

**Close Workbook 28**

**Colour**
  Background 106
  Text 106

**Column**
  Changing Width 100
  Delete 103
  Insert 102

**Count, Counta & Countblank 114**

**Copy**
  Cells 67
  Using Fill Handle 66

**Cut and Paste 69**

**Dates 97**

**Delete**
  Cell Contents 62
  Rows and Columns 103

**Display Formulas 88**

**Edit Cells 60**

**Enter**
  Numbers 35
  Text 34

**Erase Data 62**

**Excel**
  Exit 23
  Screen 10
  Start 9

**Find Text 72**

**Fonts & Font Size 94**

**Footers 84**

**Formatting 92**
  Alignment 98
  Bold, Italic & Underline 93
  Charts 129
  Dates 97
  Font & Font Size 94
  Format Painter 106
  Merge Cells 99
  Numbers 95
  Wrap Text 99

**Formulas 43**
  AutoSum 45
  Brackets 44
  Checking 47
  Display 88
  Print 88

**Freeze Panes 108**

**Functions 113**
  AutoSum 45
  Average 115
  Count, Counta & Countblank 114
  IF 117
  Maximum 116
  Minimum 116

**Headers 84**

**Help 17**
  Office Assistant 19
  What's This? 18

**Insert**
   Rows and Columns 102

**Italic 93**

**Labels**
   Alignment 98
   Enter 34

**Margins 82**

**Menus 12**

**Merge Cells 99**

**Moving Around 16**

**Office Assistant 19**

**Open Workbook 27**

**Preferences 21**

**Printing 77**
   Formulas 88
   Options 87
   Page Setup 80
   Print Preview 79
   Selection 83
   Titles 86
   Worksheet 78

**Ranges 64**
   Fill Handle 66

**Redo 63**

**Relative Addressing 118**

**Rename Worksheets 54**

**Replace Text 73**

**Revisions**
   Charts 133-134
   Creating and Saving Workbooks 40-41
   Editing 75-76
   Formatting 110-111
   Formulas 49-50
   Functions & Addressing 120-121
   Getting Started 24-25
   Open and Close Workbooks 31
   Printing 89-90
   Workbooks 58

**Rotate Text 107**

**Round 115**

**Rows**
   Changing Height 101
   Delete 103
   Insert 102

**Saving**
   In Different Formats 38
   Named Workbook 37
   New Workbook 36
   Template 39

**Scroll Bars 29**

**Sorting 74**

**Spell Checking 48**

**Starting**
   Excel 9
   New Workbook 33

**Templates**
   Saving as 39

**Text**
   Colour 106
   Entering 34
   Finding 72
   Replace 73
   Rotate 107
   Wrap 99

**Toolbars 13**

**Underline 93**

**Undo 63**

**Workbook**
   Close 28
   Multiple 30
   Open 27
   Saving Named 37
   Saving New 36
   Starting New 33
   Switching Between 53

**Worksheet**
   Checking 47
   Copying 55, 71
   Deleting 57
   Inserting 57
   Moving 55, 71
   Multiple 52
   Printing 78
   Renaming 54

**Zoom 109**

# Record of Achievement Matrix

This Matrix is to be used to measure your progress while working through the guide. This is a learning reinforcement process, you judge when you are competent.

Tick boxes are provided for each feature. 1 is for no knowledge, 2 some knowledge and 3 is for competent. A section is only complete when column 3 is completed for all parts of the section.

For details on sitting ECDL Examinations in your country please contact the local ECDL Licensee or visit the European Computer Driving Licence Foundation Limited web site at http://www.ecdl.org.

Tick the Relevant Boxes  **1**:  No Knowledge   **2**: Some Knowledge   **3**: Competent

| Section | No | Driving Lesson | 1 | 2 | 3 |
|---|---|---|---|---|---|
| **1 Getting Started** | 1 | Starting Excel | | | |
| | 2 | The Excel Screen | | | |
| | 3 | Menus | | | |
| | 4 | Toolbars | | | |
| | 5 | The Worksheet Window | | | |
| | 6 | Moving Around | | | |
| | 7 | Help | | | |
| | 8 | The Office Assistant | | | |
| | 9 | Preferences | | | |
| | 10 | Closing Excel | | | |
| **2 Open and Close Workbooks** | 13 | Opening a Workbook | | | |
| | 14 | Closing  a Workbook | | | |
| | 15 | Using Scroll Bars | | | |
| | 16 | Opening Multiple Workbooks | | | |
| **3 Creating & Saving Workbooks** | 18 | Starting a New Workbook | | | |
| | 19 | Entering Labels | | | |
| | 20 | Entering Numbers | | | |
| | 21 | Saving a New Workbook | | | |
| | 22 | Saving a Named Workbook | | | |
| | 23 | Saving in Different Formats | | | |
| | 24 | Saving as a Template | | | |
| **4 Formulas** | 27 | Formulas | | | |
| | 28 | Brackets | | | |
| | 29 | AutoSum | | | |
| | 30 | Checking for Errors | | | |
| **5 Workbooks** | 33 | Multiple Worksheets | | | |
| | 34 | Switch Between Open Workbooks | | | |
| | 35 | Renaming Sheets | | | |
| | 36 | Copying and Moving Sheets | | | |
| | 37 | Inserting and Deleting Sheets | | | |

Tick the Relevant Boxes  **1**:  No Knowledge    **2**: Some Knowledge    **3**: Competent

| Section | No | Driving Lesson | 1 | 2 | 3 |
|---|---|---|---|---|---|
| **6 Editing** | 39 | Editing Cells | | | |
| | 40 | Delete Cell Contents | | | |
| | 41 | Using Undo and Redo | | | |
| | 42 | Ranges | | | |
| | 43 | Using the Fill Handle | | | |
| | 44 | Copying Cells | | | |
| | 45 | Moving Cells | | | |
| | 46 | Copying & Moving between Workbooks | | | |
| | 47 | Finding Specific Text | | | |
| | 48 | Replacing Text | | | |
| | 49 | Sorting | | | |
| | | | | | |
| **7 Printing** | 52 | Printing | | | |
| | 53 | Print Preview | | | |
| | 54 | Page Setup | | | |
| | 55 | Margins | | | |
| | 56 | Printing a Selection | | | |
| | 57 | Headers and Footers | | | |
| | 58 | Print Titles | | | |
| | 59 | Print Options | | | |
| | 60 | Displaying and Printing Formulas | | | |
| | | | | | |
| **8 Formatting** | 63 | Formatting | | | |
| | 64 | Bold, Italic & Underline | | | |
| | 65 | Font & Font Size | | | |
| | 66 | Format Number | | | |
| | 67 | Dates | | | |
| | 68 | Alignment | | | |
| | 69 | Changing Column Width | | | |
| | 70 | Changing Row Height | | | |
| | 71 | Inserting Rows and Columns | | | |
| | 72 | Deleting Rows and Columns | | | |
| | 73 | Adding Borders | | | |
| | 74 | Adding Colour | | | |
| | 75 | Rotating Text | | | |
| | 76 | Freezing Panes | | | |
| | 77 | Zoom | | | |